Praise for *Emotionally Intelligent Living*

"This is a must-read book for those interested in gaining a better understanding of emotional intelligence. *Emotionally Intelligent Living* provides the reader with an easy-to-follow roadmap highlighting the major historical developments as well as the leading definitions and measures currently available in this field. The author has also included a rich array of innovative examples, ideas and exercises designed to improve emotionally and socially competent behaviour at home, with friends and in the workplace. She is refreshingly objective and pragmatic in presenting a number of different approaches rather than 'pushing' only one way of defining, measuring and applying emotional intelligence, which is both unique and laudable in the current EI literature. This is a very readable and straightforward how-to-do book designed to help us survive and thrive in an increasingly complex and ever-changing world. Geetu Orme is to be congratulated on a job well done."
– **Reuven Bar-On**, co-editor of *The Handbook of Emotional Intelligence*.

"In *Emotionally Intelligent Living*, Geetu Orme masterfully confronts the myth that our emotional system is a useless vestige of our evolutionary heritage and, instead, makes a persuasive case for the importance of feelings in daily interactions. Her definition of emotional intelligence as "tuning into emotions, understanding them, and taking appropriate action" represents a useful and concrete starting point for researchers and practitioners interested in appreciating how emotions colour our relationships and affect our work lives. Ms. Orme provides a helpful integration of historical and scientific approaches to the functions of human emotion and relates them to the recent proliferation of interest in emotional competencies among psychotherapists, educators, executive coaches, and organizational consultants. This is a very readable and practical book that includes a helpful guide to relevant emotional intelligence tools, exercises, and websites. I am sure I will refer to it often."
– **Peter Salovey, PhD**, Professor and Chair, Department of Psychology, Yale University.

"Geetu Orme has produced a well-written and thoughtful book on emotional intelligence. Yet, the book is more than that: it is an insight into an interesting and influential person in the field. Geetu's willingness to share her professional perspectives as well as her personal perspectives is one way in which this book shines.

Emotionally Intelligent Living is an example of Geetu's energy, focus and tenacity. It is a high-energy book that contains very useful information but is accessible and easy to read. In fact, I read it almost in one, long sitting. Geetu provides a perspective on the field that is unique and refreshing. She is using this book to promote a cause, and unlike most authors, the cause is herself! The cause is the development of important ~~
schools through Geetu's organization, Ei (UK) I
Europe in its work on emotional intelligence fo.
Geetu's efforts it will bring these same resource:

I hope that you enjoy this book as much as I did! Learn from the words in the book, but also, learn from the example of its author."
– **David Caruso, PhD.**

"The scientific literature on emotional intelligence makes two points at present, as I read it. First, emotional intelligence, defined and measured as intelligence about emotions, and intelligence enhanced by emotions, involves something brand new and independent of earlier-studied personality traits. Second, emotional intelligence, defined as such an intelligence, shows promise for explaining why some people have better human relationships than others. None of us can alter any innate part of emotional intelligence that might exist, but most of us, thank goodness, can use what we have to learn. In this book, Geetu Orme, an early and strong advocate of applying the emotional intelligence concept, has described emotional practices and provided information that can help a curious individual to develop emotional knowledge. Her book represents a welcome contribution to teachings in the area that will be valued and treasured by many readers."
– **John D. Mayer**, Department of Psychology, University of New Hampshire.

"Ms. Orme's book is terrific. It is full of clarity and possesses a fundamentally benign and optimistic view of human potential. Ms. Orme writes in a 'commonsensible' way, which is directly accessible to the reader. The whole rounded nature of the work with its self-referential quizzes, icons and so on, is also a joy. Personal anecdotes and stories from real life give extra zest to the text and point the way for everybody who is interested in realising their own potential, and improving their personal effectiveness and communication skills. I recommend this book most highly."
– **Claire Moreland**, Head, Chetham's School of Music.

"Most people haven't been well-served by books on emotional intelligence. There were a few key texts for scientists and psychologists, and there was plenty of choice for business travellers wanting something upbeat and undemanding for their journey. Geetu Orme's book changes all that. We now have a work that addresses the needs and interests of ordinary people, that doesn't over-promise or hide behind vague generalisations. Instead, she offers her readers the opportunity to use the increasingly rich body of knowledge about emotional intelligence, not for academic purposes nor for the hyperbole of business conferences, but as a means of enriching their lives. We live in world of huge potential, where, increasingly, the barriers that inhibit us come from within – from our fears, upbringing, inhibitions and lack of self-knowledge. Geetu Orme shows how the concept of emotional intelligence can be used to help us understand ourselves, combine the powers of emotion and intellect, and gradually make better choices about our lives."
– **Neil Rankin**, Editor, *Competency & Emotional Intelligence Journal*.

"As a consultant to chief executives and their management teams, I observe that all business leaders have high IQ. The distinguishing feature of the truly successful is their high EQ – their ability to understand their own intuitions and to use them constructively to lead their people. *Emotionally*

Intelligent Living introduces both the academic research and practical first steps for business leaders and their advisers to capitalise on this leadership opportunity."
– **Keith Leslie**, partner, McKinsey & Company.

"In *Emotionally Intelligent Living*, Geetu tackles some of the world's most important challenges with clarity and openness. Geetu has experienced the life changing power of attending to feelings, and has recognized that meaningful change will come only when we each commit to making small but significant changes in our daily lives. Part One addresses some of the most commonly asked questions with a strong focus on definitions and assessment. With the proliferation of assessments in this arena, readers will find value in comparisons of six of the best known tools. For me, the excitement of the book comes in Part Two where Geetu introduces specific mechanisms to re-align our personal and professional lives by tapping into the power of our hearts and minds. This tour is richly illuminated with stories and activities. Readers who are looking for support in one specific area of their lives will find it easy to turn to a chapter in Part Two and get introduced to a new perspective. The final section of the book is an engraved invitation to go further. With many appendices, lists, and annotations, Geetu sets you up for success. I am delighted to see this book come to print; our world is poised on the brink of opportunity, and perhaps more than ever before, we urgently need the kind of wisdom and humanistic vision that Geetu is encouraging.
– **Joshua Freedman**, Director of Programs, Six Seconds; co-author of *Handle With Care*.

"Geetu Orme's exciting new book provides a blueprint for leading more effective, satisfying lives by tapping into the power of emotion. The insights and practical tips in the book will be relevant to all types of people in every aspect of their lives. Geetu offers the reader compelling stories, useful exercises and enough background to put EQ to work on an everyday basis."
– **Kate Cannon**, The EQ Network.

"Voltaire says that 'Common sense is not so common'. Geetu has taken a common sense approach to a very complex subject and made it accessible and beneficial to the average person. This is a must read for all of those interested in and working in the field of emotional intelligence."
– **Lea Brovedani**, Sagacity Consulting.

"Geetu Orme effectively introduces the reader to the vast and growing field of emotional intelligence. She writes in a way that simplifies and communicates what Ei is and why it's important to our personal and professional lives. What's more, her examples and exercises allow the reader to understand and relate to Ei personally. Her comprehensive and down-to-earth style makes this accessible to the layperson as well as the professional. This is a great addition to the field!"
– **Ravi Prakash Tangri**, Chrysalis Performance Strategies Inc.

"*Emotionally Intelligent Living* represents a comprehensive approach to understanding a variety of the research and assessment tools for measuring emotional intelligence. The author discusses the confusion over what is called emotional intelligence. It is within this context that *Emotionally Intelligent Living* attempts to take what the author considers to be the best of what is available to produce a very readable book that individuals can use to help them live more emotionally intelligent lives.

Reading it one has the feeling of being at a smorgasbord with lots of different delicacies to choose from. It feels much like a conference going from session to session. What perhaps is most helpful about the book is the author's listing of tools that one can begin using immediately to live a more emotionally intelligent life. What is most enjoyable is the way the author blends anecdotal episodes from her own life experience that make you feel like you are engaged in a real dialog with the author. This book is packed with information, fun to read, and dedicated to a very worthy cause. I highly recommend it!"
– **Charles J. Wolfe**, Charles J. Wolfe Associates, LLC.

"This is a powerful book that explains and demystifies many of the concepts, ideas and workings of emotional intelligence. Using straightforward language and providing practical exercises, Geetu Orme has crafted a tool of real value and utility. *Emotionally Intelligent Living* accompanies the reader step by step through a process of learning, understanding and finally unlocking the power of emotional intelligence to help realise their full emotional potential. Emotional intelligence is perhaps a last frontier in our understanding of ourselves and the emotions and relationships that shape our lives, happiness, successes and our well-being. This book will leave you in little doubt of the potential of Ei to improve the understanding that we have of ourselves and brings powerful insights into who we are and why we behave, feel and react in the ways that we do. And in doing this, it challenges us to change our lives for the better."
– **Charles Gale.**

"*Emotionally Intelligent Living* is powerful yet practical – much like Geetu Orme herself. If there is one book you are going to read on emotional intelligence that melds cutting-edge science with practical application, this is it! A must-read from one of the pioneers in emotional intelligence."
– **Dr. J. P. Pawliw-Fry**, Co-Director, The Institute for Health & Human Potential (IHHP).

"*Emotionally Intelligent Living* will prove invaluable for those who want to work seriously with emotional intelligence. The theoretical underpinnings in combination with practical cases based on solid EQ experience will be enormously useful. The book will be a guide that both advances our thinking on emotional intelligence and gives us practical and down to earth exercises to work with."
– **Dr. Margareta Sjölund**, CEO, Kandidata, Stockholm.

Emotionally Intelligent Living

Geetu Orme

Illustrations by Jan Johnston

Crown House Publishing
www.crownhouse.co.uk

First published in the UK by

Crown House Publishing Limited
Crown Buildings
Bancyfelin
Carmarthen
Wales
SA33 5ND
UK

www.crownhouse.co.uk

British Library Cataloguing-in-Publication Data
A catalogue entry for this book is available
from the British Library.

ISBN 1899836470

Printed and bound in the UK by
Bell & Bain Limited, Glasgow

All information current at time of going to print. The author and Crown House
Publishing cannot be held responsible for any information that is inaccurate. The views
on emotional intelligence are the author's own, based on her work and experience as a
practitioner in the field of emotional intelligence, working with individuals and teams to
measure and develop their emotional intelligence.

For my niece Shakti

You are energy in both name and spirit

The author is donating the proceeds from this book to fund projects on emotional intelligence in the education, health and voluntary sectors.

'I want to beg you, as much as I can, to be patient toward all that is unsolved in your heart and to try to love the questions themselves like locked rooms and like books that are written in a very foreign tongue. Do not seek the answers, which cannot be given to you because you would not be able to live them. And the point is to live everything. Live the questions now. Perhaps you will then gradually, without noticing it, live along some distant day into the answer.'

Rainer Maria Rilke (1875–1926)

Table of Contents

Appendices

Foreword

Being whole, being all that we can be is one of the greatest challenges facing people today. Whether we struggle to juggle home, family and work or the thousand and one other demands on our time and on our lives, we are looking for answers, we want and demand more from our lives. What was fine for our parents and our grand parents is not enough. For many this sense of dissatisfaction gradually creeps up, until we are overwhelmed or until we simply cannot cope any more.

The pressures of modern living leads many people to leave their jobs, their partners or their families; for others it leads to the search for the elusive work-life balance. Emotional intelligence is about combining the strengths of the rational brain and mind with the insight, intuition and gut instinct of our emotions. It is not about the triumph of rational thought over the emotional self, but about combining strengths of both to be whole, to be the best we can be.

Much can be revealed about what we say, the language we use and the way we communicate. For instance, we often talk of being ruled by our heads not our hearts, yet as this book demonstrates, decision making has as much to do with our emotions as our logic. For some of us, logic and rational argument serve as a means to justify decisions we have already made based on intuition or emotion. For others, we don't have the time to weigh up all the options or, at other times, we have strong intuitive knowledge that one path is better than the other.

But what is going on here? Is emotional intelligence just another fad or just more airport lounge pop-psychology to fill the book shelves and help us pass the time as we travel our busy lives seeking something we know not what?

Perhaps or perhaps not, but to quote Arthur Schopenhauer, philosopher:

> 'All truth passes through 3 phases: first, it is ridiculed, second, it is violently opposed. Third, it is accepted as being self evident.'

However, drawing on the vast reservoir of research and writing on emotional intelligence, Geetu Orme has brought together a unique book which guides the reader with practical exercises and examples. This work takes us on an intellectual journey as well as an emotional one; it allows the mind to comprehend what is going on for us emotionally – it helps to bring emotional issues into conscious awareness where they can be looked at and dealt with.

Call it what you like, we all use this advanced common sense to navigate our lives, but by being aware of our emotions as well as our thoughts and by bringing this understanding into our consciousness we can more effectively manage our lives.

For us to accept something we must first understand it. Through exercises and practical, easy to grasp explanations, Geetu Orme brings emotional intelligence alive and provides more of us with greater access to the subject and by extension to a greater understanding of ourselves.

If this book helps you to a better understanding of yourself, by throwing some light on your patterns and your habits, then it has done its job and done it well. If it further serves to stimulate the debate and inspire others to investigate the true potential in all of us then even better.

John Weston
Director of Director Development
Institute of Directors
London

Glossary

amygdala	The part of the emotional brain where all memories that have emotional significance are housed.
'amygdala hijack'	The term used by Daniel Goleman to describe 'emotional flooding' where the emotional brain (triggered by memories) creates a strong flood of emotion in the brain – leading to a fight or flight reaction (usually fight) often in response to threat.
cortex	The thinking part of the brain.
DHEA (dehydroepiandrosterone)	The hormone associated with anti-ageing, in the USA, known as the 'elixir of youth'. It can be naturally generated in the body through activating positive emotions like appreciation and love. It is a precursor to testosterone in men and oestrogen in women.
hippocampus	The part of the emotional brain which compares the information coming in with what is stored in our emotional memories. The information then gets relayed either to the cortex for thinking or to the *amygdala* for initiating a fight/flight reaction.
instrument	In this context, used to refer to a questionnaire or test that measures emotional intelligence.
inventory	The term used for the Bar-On EQ-i self-assessment published by Multi-Health Systems (see Chapter 3 for details, and Appendix 3). People balked at the term 'test' since it denoted right or wrong.
oxymoron	The word for two contradictory terms encountered together, when they seem to contradict one another – e.g. bittersweet, sweet sorrow, emotional intelligence.
quotient	Mathematically, this refers to the result of the division of one number by another. It is used in the context of 'Intelligence Quotient' and 'Emotional Quotient' to indicate that actual scores are used to define your level of IQ and EQ.

synaesthesia	This is the process of imagining what feelings look like, taste like or smell like – in other words, engaging our senses with feelings. It is a process that is used in the Multifactor Emotional Intelligence Scale (MEIS) to test ability to use emotions (see Chapter 4).
'360 degree feedback, 360 degree measure'	A term used to refer to the process of getting information about yourself from other people. There are 360 degrees in a full circle, so usually it means that people from many different parts of your life contribute their views, in this case in the form of ratings of your emotional intelligence.

Introduction

'Too many people are having near-life experiences.'

I believe that emotional intelligence represents the most important set of skills that we need to develop in order to survive as a human race, and experience life to the full. Most of the world is still unaware of emotional intelligence and its potential influence on how we live, teach and work, even though the concept has been around for decades.

My intention in this book is to explain emotional intelligence in an accessible way. As we move into a future that is increasingly uncertain, difficult and potentially stressful, our emotional intelligence will determine who succeeds and who doesn't, who lives a life of pain and who copes, who is happy and who is miserable, who has long-term relationships and who lives in solitude. Some people have referred to emotional intelligence as 'advanced common sense'. I aim to explore the myths and truths about it.

Until now, the many clinicians, psychologists and academics who conduct important research in this field have not been able to communicate their message succinctly and powerfully. The salient points have been hidden in language that is technical and complex. Yet everyone stands to benefit from taking on board the concept of emotional intelligence. Wherever you live in the world, in whatever circumstances, whatever job you do, however much money you earn, there is information in this book that will be useful to you. It's designed to be free of jargon, and any terms used that might be interpreted as 'borderline' jargon are explained in the Glossary on the previous pages.

Researchers have found that there is something other than our cognitive intelligence (or IQ) that makes a difference to our success and happiness in life – emotional intelligence is what accounts for this difference. In a nutshell, *Emotionally Intelligent Living* is about living fully and happily. It involves taking an honest look at your day-to-day life. The book uses the concepts of emotional intelligence to give you a language for focusing on what is important to you. This reflection may not always be comfortable but I have tried to make it as pain-free as possible with clear guidance on what to do and how to do it.

My promise is that you will discover:

- what emotional intelligence is
- why it matters to you
- how you can measure your own emotional intelligence
- how you can address emotionally challenging situations in your life to achieve greater happiness.

It will be an exciting and fun journey. You will also be able to recall your own examples of high and low emotional intelligence, and you will see your own life reflected in the stories you read here.

You might think that this book offers an easy formula – a quick fix for all your emotional needs and life problems. Not quite! The ideas contained here may provide you with a long-term shift in your awareness of emotions in day-to-day life. For instance, you may have wanted for a while to make some adjustments in your day-to-day life in order to be happier or more at ease – this book will give you practical steps to start a process of personal change. Or, it could provide more of a *reflective* experience for you – an opportunity for you to think about what is working in your life and also what you want to change. I encourage you to engage wholeheartedly with the activities in the book by working through them and completing them, rather than just thinking about them, in order to gain the greatest personal value.

If you want to get to the bottom of the essential points about emotional intelligence, this book is the place to start. Here you will find an outline of the key research and background information as well as practical ways to increase your emotional intelligence. If you are undertaking research in this field or choose to delve deeper, the Bibliography will point you in the right direction to find the detailed analytical background and the scientific research.

The main part of the book is divided into three parts. **Part 1** gives the background, focusing on what emotional intelligence is, the underpinning science of emotional intelligence, the current schools of thought on emotional intelligence and how to measure it. At the end of Part 1, you will have the opportunity to complete a short test of your own emotional intelligence and a questionnaire on how you are feeling in different parts of your life. This will help pinpoint the main chapters you need to focus on in Parts 2 and 3.

Part 2 starts to apply the concepts of emotional intelligence to your personal life – particularly to yourself, family, friends, and partner relationships. **Part 3** focuses on the workplace – particularly, how emotional intelligence relates to your career, working in teams, leadership, and making decisions. Each chapter in these two parts contains examples of high and low emotional intelligence and two key activities for you to work through.

All the stories of high and low emotional intelligence are from my own life and from the lives of those close to me. (All first names have been changed.) In these stories I believe you will see your own experiences reflected, together with your own memories of great times and not-so-happy times. They are there to bring the theory to life and to provide background learning to the concepts.

The following icons are used to signpost different features:

to indicate where we are going in a new chapter

a definition

where research is quoted

a real-life story that illustrates low or high emotional intelligence an activity, test or quiz.

Emotionally Intelligent Living is designed to encourage you to reflect on what is really happening in your life – to take action in areas that are out of balance or where you may want more emotional intelligence in order to feel happier and more balanced. By the end of this book, you will be able to take action in those areas where you see yourself needing 'renewal'.[i]

Good luck with your journey. There is, of course, no fixed destination – you yourself decide where you want to end up. This book invites you to start a conversation with yourself about your life that will spur you to action. Without the conversation there will be no change. As Henry Fonda said in the film *Twelve Angry Men*, "No one has to change but everyone must have the conversation."

---

[i] Dr Steve Stein, CEO of Multi-Health Systems in Canada, used this term during a recent workshop on the Bar-On Emotional Quotient Inventory to describe personal weaknesses (Cheshire, September 2000).

Part 1

Background

'The intuitive mind is a sacred gift
and the rational mind
is a faithful servant.
We have created a society
that honours the servant
and has forgotten the gift.'
Albert Einstein (1879–1955)

Chapter 1

What is Emotional Intelligence?

This chapter covers:

- Seven 'myths' about emotional intelligence
- Some definitions of emotional intelligence
- Being emotionally intelligent, day to day
- Three ways of looking at 'your house'
- Overview of the activities included in this book
- Two key features of emotional intelligence – being emotionally intelligent and making emotionally intelligent choices
- Key points about emotional intelligence
- A brief history of the research into emotional intelligence.

Have you ever wondered why it is that some people just seem to get on with life and have a happy time while others seem to struggle and are unable to achieve what they want? Why is it that people from a similar social or academic background end up with dramatically different lives? How is it that when we meet fellow travellers on a bus, train or plane, we get an instant feel for whether or not we want to spend time with them? We make decisions consciously and unconsciously about how much 'work' it will take to get to know someone and whether or not we want to.

How is it that faced with the same event – for instance, redundancy or a change in health – two people react so differently? One of them might put it down to bad luck or 'time for a change', while the other might violently resent what has happened and blame themselves or the people around them, perhaps for years.

It always fascinates me how two people from the same family can have contrasting 'fates' when it comes to happy, satisfying, loving relationships. Even people from the same background and family circumstances can have very different ways of coping with life, traumatic events and their relationships.

How can two people of the same age sometimes look so different – one looking ten years younger than the other? In Chapter 2 on the science underpinning emotional intelligence, you will discover the role of positive emotions in helping us to stay healthy and youthful.

Whilst each of us has our own unique experience of life, there are abilities we can learn – such as how to manage our emotions so that we produce sufficient quantities of the 'anti-ageing' hormone (DHEA), or how to identify accurately how we are feeling so that we can take steps to move closer to what we really want. These abilities are what is captured by the term *emotional intelligence*.

Myths About Emotional Intelligence

A whole range of articles, books and research papers has been published in recent years – some serious, some light-hearted – and a number of myths have arisen surrounding the topic of emotional intelligence. Let's explore some of these.

Myth	My view
Myth No. 1: *There is no place for emotions in this life; facts are more solid and useful.*	Emotions are present day and night. We can't stop ourselves from feeling. Our connection to others is emotional and emotions give us useful information on what is really happening. By focusing on emotions, we can actually deal with facts quicker, more easily and more effectively.
Myth No. 2: *Emotional intelligence involves telling everyone how you feel. It could be particularly career-limiting if you cry at work, or it could end your personal relationships if you tell people close to you how you really feel about them.*	Sometimes emotional intelligence involves expressing emotion, but, more often than not, it's about *managing emotion* so that you don't allow your own or other people's emotions to overwhelm you. So being emotionally intelligent doesn't necessarily involve telling everyone how you feel. Sometimes it involves being able to know for yourself how you feel and then finding the most appropriate way to communicate this to someone else.
Myth No. 3: *Emotional intelligence means more hugging and touching than usual and I don't want to get accused of sexual harassment.*	Sometimes expressing emotion can involve a physical element – a touch on the hand, a comforting hug – but emotional intelligence is not a licence to touch someone when they don't want to be touched. In fact, this could be considered to be very emotionally *un*intelligent in certain situations.
Myth No. 4: *Focusing on emotions takes time – I'm too busy to find out what people feel.*	If you don't find out what people feel, you may spend longer focused on the 'wrong things' than the right things. Negative emotions are difficult obstacles and positive emotions help to get the job done. It may not necessarily take more time; it's simply about where you choose to focus your attention – on emotions, or on thoughts.
Myth No. 5: *My feelings and emotions are invisible to others.*	This is blissful ignorance. People are incredibly perceptive and can subconsciously pick up on when the words don't match the body language. We all have the ability to notice emotions.

contd.

Myth	My view
Myth No. 6: *We should only focus on positive emotions, not on negative ones.*	There is much truth in this statement, from a health perspective (see Chapter 2). But even negative emotions can be a signal that something needs to change – see **Activity 11** in the chapter on careers (Chapter 9). Negative emotions are a part of life, so it's useful to learn how to deal with them and to distinguish the ones that can be the most debilitating if we let them in.
Myth No. 7: *Emotional intelligence is another 'pop psychology' term which has nothing new to offer.*	Emotional intelligence does define a set of skills and abilities much needed in schools and business. Knowledge of emotional intelligence should influence what we teach at school, how we run companies, how we live day-to-day in our families. Whilst the concept has been around for years, there are now more people working at the 'ground level' to help teach these skills and the techniques for measuring it and developing it in ourselves and in others.[i]

A great deal of misinformation about what emotional intelligence is has so far served to keep the concept in the hands of a small group of people. Through this book I intend to address this problem and educate a wider audience about emotional intelligence.

Defining Emotional Intelligence

At the time of writing, there is a company in Canada that promotes 'emotionally intelligent' dolls,[ii] and another company has just started selling internet greeting cards with feelings.[iii] What does being 'emotional intelligent' mean? This is my simple definition:

Being emotionally intelligent involves tuning into emotions, understanding them and taking appropriate action.

The three elements in my definition involve both our own emotions and those of others:

- **tuning into** the emotions of ourselves and others
- **understanding** emotions in ourselves and others
- **taking appropriate action** on the emotional content that we find.

I use the continuous tense (*being, taking,* etc.) in my definition, because it's something that we are ideally doing in every experience, in every conversation. But being emotionally intelligent applies not just to how we meet our day-to-day life experiences but also our life's crises – job redundancy, divorce, bereavement, major disputes, and so on.

Dr. David Caruso, co-creator of the Multifactor Emotional Intelligence Scale (MEIS), has offered another definition: 'Emotional intelligence is the ability to use your emotions to help you solve problems and live a more effective life. Emotional intelligence without intelligence, or intelligence without emotional intelligence, is only part of a solution. The complete solution is the head working with the heart.'

Other definitions can be found in Appendix 1.

I mentioned earlier that some people perceive emotional intelligence to be about 'advanced common sense'.[iv] In many ways, common sense is exactly what emotional intelligence is – some people have large amounts of common sense without even knowing that there is a thing called 'emotional intelligence'. They just seem to know what to do in the heat of the moment. Sometimes the actions we take reflect the way we are dealing with our own emotions, sometimes they show how we are dealing with other people's emotions. Sometimes it's obvious and sometimes not so obvious. Emotional intelligence – that ability to **tune into** emotions, **understand** them and **take appropriate action** – adds up to *advanced* common sense. The study of emotional intelligence provides us with a framework and some easy-to-learn steps for using our advanced common sense: knowing what to do in a particular situation and doing it.

Being Emotionally Intelligent Day to Day

When you are having a conversation with a friend, are you **tuned into** how you and they are feeling? Do you **understand** why you feel what you do? Do you **act** in line with these feelings? When you are feeling sad, do you **take action** to make life better for yourself or do you tend to sit in sadness for hours? In situations where it would be better to be happy, are you able to '**turn on**' this feeling so that it can help you deal with a particular situation? Are you resilient and able to cope with life crises? Or are you needy, wanting attention from others? These are big questions, I know, but they all have to do with your emotional intelligence. This is best illustrated with some stories.

Four female friends were all excited about their trip to Hawaii. This was going to be their first holiday away together in a long time. Kristy's husband worked as a pilot for a major airline so it allowed them to buy discount tickets that made the trip possible. When they left from their home town they were chatting happily about leaving the cold drizzly weather and lying on a warm sandy beach in beautiful Hawaii. They could almost taste the Pina Coladas before they left home! The first bump happened when they had to disembark before taking their connecting flight. They knew that part of the 'deal' of their inexpensive tickets was their 'stand-by' status – this meant that they could only fly if seats were available. They were told that it was unlikely that they would get a flight out until the following morning. Kristy noticed the downcast look of her friends and suggested they go on a hunt for the best bar or nightclub in town. Her infectious mood caught on with two of the other girls. They laughed as they flipped through the phone book looking for an exciting place to spend the evening. The fourth friend, Donna was upset that the others had not noticed her when she had walked away to sit by herself. When the others approached her to leave and find a taxi, she was annoyed "I'm not going, this is a disaster, we may as well all go home; the trip has been ruined!" They were finally able to persuade her to join them, but she spent the entire evening sulking – she responded to all questions with one word answers. Eventually, they were able to get a room at a hotel close to the airport so first thing in the morning they were back at the airport waiting for a flight out. When they were on the plane to Hawaii, Donna's mood did not improve. Having determined that the trip was spoiled by one small hiccup in the travel plans, she spent the rest of her holiday finding fault with everything. Kristy realised that Donna could only 'ruin' their vacation if they allowed her to. When she went to the beach, she moved away from Donna and found people with whom she could laugh and enjoy herself. By the end of the week, the other two were feeling Donna's sour mood and although they tried not to let her negatively affect their holiday, they felt relieved when they arrived back home. Donna's perception of their one setback as a 'disaster' allowed her to create the reality of the 'ruined vacation'.

So, who had the ability to manage their emotions and those of others? Sometimes it's easy to manage our own emotions when we are feeling good (for instance, Kristy staying upbeat and enthusiastic about the holiday) but how well did she manage the emotions of Donna? You may be interested to know that Donna and Kristy are no longer friends; low emotional intelligence sometimes costs relationships. Kristy probably did her best in the situation, but she wasn't able to bring Donna round – consequently, Donna's bad mood affected everyone and their enjoyment of the holiday.

Let's look at another example. It concerns Andrew, who has been in his new job for under two weeks. Before this job he was the head of division in a well-known consumer company. He then travelled the world, and on his return, he took a part-time job as a researcher to earn some cash while he considered broader career options.

This job is quite different to anything he has ever experienced. For one, he has always been around people who have been younger than him and more junior. Just days into a new role, he is already doubting his confidence and abilities. Andrew is working under a boss who does not value his contribution – someone who is aggressive and finds fault with everything that Andrew and other people do. He does not seem to have a nice thing to say about anyone.

Emotionally Unintelligent Response:

Andrew begins to feel worthless in his new position, blames the boss, and talks about him behind his back to other colleagues. He continues to find fault with himself, doubts his ability and lets these feelings affect his work and his relationship with his boss. He does not acknowledge the emotions that he, and his boss, must be feeling, and does not take action to address them. By gossiping behind his boss's back and saying nothing to him directly, he is not achieving a positive outcome.

Emotionally Intelligent Response:

Andrew tunes in to the fact that the uncomfortable feelings that he is having are a problem for him, his colleagues and for his boss. He understands that his reaction to the situation is partly based on his experiences and memories of working with more effective bosses. He recognises his instant dislike for people who exert autocratic authority and he identifies that in reacting to his boss, he is remembering a number of old memories (not just the current one). He is able to size up how much of the situation is real and how much is 'dreamed up' and exaggerated. He is able to work out what the current situation is costing him (e.g. low self confidence, low energy, reduced satisfaction with work). He can weigh up whether it is appropriate to confront the situation with his boss or change job. Andrew decides that simply stopping blaming others and himself will make life better for him in the short term. Just by doing this, his boss adjusts his behaviour. This simple action on Andrew's part helps him to understand how to be a better manager.

In summary, Andrew's emotionally intelligent response entails: **being aware** of his emotions; **recognising** what he is feeling; being **objective** about his emotions; putting his feelings and his situation **in context**; **acting positively** on the information he gains from his emotions; **learning** from his emotions.

Three Ways of Looking at 'Your House'

Another way to think about emotional intelligence is by imagining yourself as a house, and looking at three aspects – people, inner workings, and bad weather.

People

Do people come to visit your house? Do they enjoy it when they are there? Does your house stay intact when others are around or is it mayhem?

Are you able to connect with other people, by sensing what is happening and using emotion to build bonds? Do you leave conversations feeling good about yourself, or less good? Do you express what you really feel when you're with other people? Do you **tune into** what is happening? Emotional intelligence is about the relationships we have with others and the quality of our interactions with others. For example, when you're with people do you give energy to others or do you deplete their energy? In the story you have just read, did people want to come to visit Donna in her house of bad mood, anger and upset for things that were outside anyone's control? Clearly Donna was not good at dealing with the other people around her, particularly given that the situation – a holiday – was meant to be enjoyable and upbeat.

11

Inner Workings

Do you know how your house functions – its heating system, its plumbing? Do you know what lies underneath the floors and behind the walls?

Do you **understand** the basics of your own emotions – how you're feeling and why? Emotional intelligence is about understanding our own inner workings – how we think, how we feel. It is necessary to understand our own before we can start to read emotions in other people. Did Donna understand why she felt as badly as she felt, and the impact she was having on her friends? Did she know what the issue was really about? Was she jealous of Kristy for having a husband who could get discounted air tickets?

Bad Weather

When there is bad weather and your house is flooded, or struck by lightning, or if there's a power cut late in the evening, do you know what to do?

How do you deal with emotions in tough situations? Do you explode, or go under, or do you cope and take things in your stride? Do you **take action** in line with what is needed? There is little time in a crisis to assess priorities and protect dependants. Emotional intelligence is about dealing with our emotions and those of other people even in tough situations. How did Donna react when things didn't go her way? Clearly she wasn't able to deal with her own emotions, even in a minor crisis.

Overview of Activities Included in this Book

This book includes several activities for you to do. The table below indicates how each activity links with the three aspects of our 'house' image – *people, inner workings* and *bad weather*. It may help you to prioritise your reading of the book – for instance, if you're particularly keen to work on how you cope with 'bad weather' (or difficult situations), you could concentrate on activities flagged in the final column.

No.	Activity	Chapter	People	Inner workings	Bad weather
1	Quick assessment of your emotional intelligence using MEIS	4	✓	✓	✓
2	Feelings assessment	4	✓	✓	
3	Your life seen from a helicopter	5	✓	✓	✓
4	Charting your moods	5		✓	
5	Using TV to increase emotional intelligence	6	✓	✓	✓
6	Seeing modern art	6	✓	✓	
7	TRUST your friend	7	✓	✓	✓
8	Fun fantasies	7	✓		
9	Mismanaged anger	8	✓	✓	✓
10	Step up	8	✓	✓	✓
11	Is your career safe?	9	✓	✓	✓
12	Taking action	9	✓	✓	✓
13	Validation and invalidation	10	✓	✓	✓
14	Team talk	10	✓	✓	✓
15	Helping others to know you	11	✓	✓	
16	Cost/benefit analysis	11	✓	✓	✓
17	Planting time	12	✓	✓	✓
18	EBC analysis	12	✓	✓	✓

Features of Emotional Intelligence

There are two features of emotional intelligence worth exploring. For me, they differentiate it from other frameworks of development.

1. Being Emotionally Intelligent

My definition of emotional intelligence starts with the word 'being'. This is an important aspect of emotional intelligence. Let's look at the definition again.

Being** emotionally intelligent involves **tuning into** emotions, **understanding** them and **taking appropriate action.

Many people have defined emotional intelligence by describing what people *do*, usually in the form of lists of behaviours or actions. My experience is that it is how someone is *being* that makes the most difference. In other words, even without going through a formal assessment of your emotional intelligence, how you are *being* in a particular situation will determine how emotionally intelligent you really are.

The following reflection activity will help to explain this concept.[v]

Three components for success

(a) Write down the names of three people who you regard as being exceptional – they could be dead or alive, famous or known to you personally. Write these in the first column.

(b) Now write down the qualities that made them exceptional. Write these in the second column, each on a separate line. (E.g. committed, loyal, generous, self-sacrificing, caring, confident, hard-working, knowledgeable, able to forgive, considerate, kind, gentle, clear, determined, unflappable.)

(c) Now put a K, D or B next to the qualities, using the following key:

- K: Qualities that involve knowledge
- D: Qualities that are about the actions they take – things you can see these people doing
- B: Qualities that are about how they actually are, or how they are being.

e.g. committed – B, loyal – B, generous – B, self-sacrificing – B, caring – B, confident – B, hard-working – B, technical knowledge – K, forgiving – D/B, considerate – B, kind – B, gentle – B, clear – B, determined – B, unflappable – B, keep in touch – D, communicator – D, know what to say – K

Names of exceptional people	Their qualities	K, D or B

I'm sure that most of the qualities you listed are how your chosen people are *being* (B) – emotional intelligence is not just about knowing what to do and doing it, it's how you are *being* as you go about the knowing and doing that makes the difference. As has often been said, we are human beings, not human doings.

2. Making Emotionally Intelligent Choices

Whilst I have met many skilled and capable people over the years, my belief is that many people who have high potential for emotional intelligence may not always make emotionally intelligent choices in the heat of the moment. Emotional intelligence involves not only knowing what to do and *being* it, it's also about doing the best thing *when it matters*. It's not just about tuning into emotions when you are feeling joy, passion, or love for those around you – it's also about being able to face disruptive emotions like anger and fear and making choices when you're in the middle of a crisis. Given that our brains are wired up for letting our emotions rule us (for instance, triggering strong physiological reactions when there is a hint of threat – see Chapter 2), then it's easy to see how this is likely to be more of a learned ability, rather than one we are born with.

Key Points about Emotional Intelligence

So why is it important that we understand what emotional intelligence is? Are there different kinds of emotional intelligence? Is there a difference between men and women, or between people of different ages, or people doing different kinds of job? The key information summarised below is the result of many studies, documented in books, research papers and case studies during the last twenty years. The most important of these are listed in the Bibliography.

Emotional intelligence can be learned and developed. There are now a variety of different ways to teach and learn about emotional intelligence. Whatever your current level of emotional intelligence, with the right support, activities and commitment, you can improve it. Unlike your cognitive intelligence (or IQ), which peaks at age seventeen and stays constant throughout most of your life until it declines in old age, your emotional intelligence can be improved at any age in life.

Emotional intelligence increases with life experience. Research by Dr. Reuven Bar-On, using a measure of emotional intelligence called the Emotional Quotient Inventory (EQ-i), confirms that emotional intelligence increases with age, peaks in the age group forty to forty-nine and then levels out.[vi] This could imply that after the age of forty-nine few new experiences add to or enhance our emotional intelligence. However, I prefer to think that learning about ourselves is a lifelong task. Research using the Multifactor Emotional Intelligence Scale (MEIS) also suggests that emotional intelligence improves with age, increasing between young adolescence and early adulthood.[vii]

Everyone's emotional intelligence needs are different. We all live among other people – in our family, community or place of work – and being able to understand, interpret and use the emotional content of life is useful for all of us. However, different jobs may require different levels of emotional intelligence.[viii] They even require different aspects of emotional intelligence – for instance, if you work in a job which involves a high degree of contact with other people, you may need more of an ability to manage emotions (to deal with the storms), whereas if you are a counsellor, you may need a higher ability to understand your own emotions.

There are some differences between men and women. When Reuven Bar-On's Emotional Quotient Inventory was used in a study of 7,700 men and women it was found that, whilst there was no difference between men and women on total EQ (or Emotional Quotient), women scored higher on all three *interpersonal* abilities (empathy, interpersonal relationship and social responsibility) and men scored higher on *intrapersonal* dimensions (e.g. self-actualisation, assertiveness), *stress management* (stress tolerance, impulse control) and *adaptability* (e.g. reality-testing, problem-solving). According to Dr. Bar-On, "Women are more aware of emotions, demonstrate more empathy, relate better interpersonally, and act more socially responsible than men; on the other hand, men appear to have better self-regard, are more independent, cope better with stress, are more flexible, solve problems better, and are more optimistic than women."[ix]

Being emotionally intelligent adds to your general intelligence. Whether you're being systematic about buying your groceries in a supermarket, or being organised about setting and achieving a business plan, or even your life goals, you need a good IQ (intelligence quotient).[x] When solving a problem, being realistic about what is achievable involves some practical knowledge. Focusing on emotional intelligence doesn't mean throwing out the guidelines and structures that you learned a long time ago to help organise your day-to-day life. An awareness of the *emotional* aspects of what is happening will add to the abilities measured by IQ. As the psychologist David Wechsler put it in 1940, 'individuals with identical IQs may differ very markedly in regard to their effective ability to cope with the environment.'[xi]

'Emotional intelligence' is not an oxymoron. An oxymoron is a word or phrase that brings together two contradictory ideas (such as 'bittersweet', 'living death'). Within what might appear a contradiction, 'emotional intelligence', lies the depth of the concept of EI – it involves *both* the process of tuning into your emotions (sometimes regarded as the 'soft' stuff) *and* the need to be analytical about emotions and learn new skills in a 'hard' analytical way. Since 1990, when John Mayer and Peter Salovey coined the term 'emotional intelligence', their work, and that of David Caruso, has highlighted this important combination of thinking and feeling. Both are necessary if you are to make good decisions.

Emotional intelligence has some hard science underpinning it. In the next chapter, you can read about the essential learning points from the fields of neurology, medicine and psychology. Medical and scientific breakthroughs have added to our understanding of emotions and the role of emotions in staying healthy.

Emotional intelligence affects our ability to make decisions. We make most of our decisions through our emotions, whether we think so or not. So emotional intelligence is useful for making good decisions. Chapter 2 on 'The underpinning science' and chapter 12 on 'Making decisions' will explore this further.

Emotional intelligence is reflected in relationships. This is the area where you generally observe, at close hand, people with high emotional intelligence – they tend to enjoy close relationships, and are comfortable with themselves and with others.

Emotional intelligence can be measured. There is now a range of different measures of emotional intelligence (see Chapter 3 and

Appendices 2 and 3). In addition, numerous studies have been conducted which prove that a focus on emotional intelligence has benefits to health, business success, and relationships.[xii] Particularly useful are the case studies documented by HeartMath Europe on the benefits of their one-day workshops on Inner Quality Management. The benefits they found include reduced blood pressure, higher levels of personal productivity and team effectiveness[xiii] – and these benefits are sustained six months after people are taught tools which are part of the HeartMath system. (Chapter 2 covers the HeartMath system.)

A Brief History of Research into Emotional Intelligence

As David Caruso has pointed out, we have come a long way since 100 B.C.E. when the poet/philosopher Publius Syrus said, 'Rule your feelings lest your feelings rule you.' Today there is a growing body of professionals around the world – teachers, counsellors, psychologists, consultants and trainers, who are specialists in emotional intelligence. So what is the sequence of events that has made emotional intelligence such an important and popular concept?[1]

1920　The earliest studies on what has now come to be known as emotional intelligence date back to the 1920s, to research conducted by **Robert Thorndike**. His work focused on identifying what makes up 'intelligence' and indicated that 'social intelligence' was a part of general intelligence. He defined social intelligence as 'the abilities to understand others and to act or behave wisely in relation to others'.[xiv] During his time, other researchers dismissed his suggestion that 'social intelligence' might be an important capability to develop in the school system. This was far ahead of its time

---

[1] The term emotional intelligence was in fact used in the 1950s but without particular scientific relevance. Most of the researchers and academics mentioned here researched aspects of 'intelligence' rather than 'emotional intelligence'. In their time, they did not mention anything explicit about emotional intelligence or its measure. Some of these academics have made links between their early work and emotional intelligence. The history presented here is a list of the academics and theorists that the Author believes provided the most significant study of what is now known as 'emotional intelligence'.

– children were 'best seen and not heard' at this time, and were not encouraged to sit together to develop close friendships. It was nearly fifteen years before other researchers continued this early work.

1935   **Edgar Doll**, an Australian psychologist, devised a structured interview called the Vineland Social Maturity Scale to assess social competence, which gave an SQ (social quotient) score to indicate the level of social maturity of the individual.[xv] It was forty-five years later that a clinical psychologist, Reuven Bar-On, pursued this line of research.

1940   **David Wechsler** continued to challenge the traditional view on intelligence with his notion of 'non intellective intelligence'. He was the first researcher to indicate that there was a range of intelligences, other than traditional IQ, that were part of general intelligence. Yet his name has been associated with a known test for IQ – the Wechsler Intelligence Scale.

1948   **R. W. Leeper** made a small but important contribution to the early work of David Wechsler, in studying 'emotional thought'. He found that emotions 'arouse, sustain and direct activity'.[xvi] He proposed that 'emotional thought' was part of, and contributes to, 'logical thought' and intelligence in general.[xvii] It was another thirty-five years before Howard Gardner helped to broaden the view of aspects of 'intelligence' in the twentieth century.

1973   **Peter Sifneos** coined the term 'alexithymia' (from the Greek – *a* meaning absence, *lexis* meaning word, *thymos* meaning feelings, i.e. an absence of words for feelings). This is a condition best described as the opposite of emotional intelligence – it includes difficulty *identifying* feelings; difficulty *distinguishing* between different feelings, both in words and in the sensations created in the body; difficulty in *imagining* feelings and difficulty in *describing* them to others.

1980   **Reuven Bar-On**, a clinical psychologist, started to research the question 'Why is it that some people achieve overall emotional health and wellbeing whilst others don't?'[xviii] His initial doctoral research was in South Africa, later in Israel. During the 1980s and 1990s he worked directly on measuring emotional intelligence using his instrument, the Emotional Quotient Inventory (EQ-i), in over fifteen different countries. In 1985 he coined the term 'emotional quotient' (EQ).

1983 **Howard Gardner**, a professor at Harvard University, found that one could categorise a number of different intelligences. He defined seven initially and more recently added an eighth and ninth: spatial/visual, linguistic, intrapersonal, musical, bodily/kinaesthetic, interpersonal and logical; naturist and existential were added in 1998.

1985 **Robert Sternberg** continued the research started by Doll, Wechsler and Leeper. He asked people to describe an 'intelligent' person and in his findings the concept of 'practical intelligence' emerged.

 He wrote: 'Practical intelligence is the ability to adapt to, change or alter real-life situations.'[xix] This research created a broader view of intelligence.

1985 **Peter Salovey** and **John Mayer** met at Yale University where John was speaking about his post-doctorate research at Stanford University on cognition and affect. This was when they started to pull together the isolated phrases, ideas and research areas into a coherent whole. They were influenced by early work on emotions and the role of thinking in emotions.[2]

---

[2] John Mayer states that the following published works most contributed to the idea of emotional intelligence:

Alloy & Abramson's work on depressive realism (1979, 1988).
James Averill's works on constructivism in emotion (1970) and on emotional creativity (1992).
Frijda's works on the laws of emotion (1988).
Jung's work on the feeling function in cognition (1920).
Schwarz and Clore's work on the informative function of emotion (1988).
Mayer's work on the role of emotion in creativity and thinking (1986).
Payne's work which explicitly uses the term 'emotional intelligence' (1986).
Taylor's work on alexithymia (1984).

Source: Jack Mayer. Personal e-mail. March 2001.

1990   **John Mayer** and **Peter Salovey** published their first research paper, in which they coined the term 'emotional intelligence', defined it and provided the first scientific measure of emotional intelligence. Their early definition of emotional intelligence was: 'The ability to monitor one's own and others' feelings and emotions, to discriminate among them, and to use this information to guide one's thinking and action.'[xx] In the same year, they published their first review of emotional intelligence. Two years previously, they had been discussing the recent local elections in their state and wondering how Gary Hart, the Democratic candidate, who was the front-runner in the elections, had lost the faith of the electorate when a scandal broke out about his extra-marital affair. They had wondered how such an intelligent individual could orchestrate his own destruction.[xxi] After their 1990 paper, they published subsequent papers in 1993 and 1995 and have spoken about their work at many conferences. By now, it had already been eleven years since Jack Mayer had met David Caruso, who later joined Mayer and Salovey to create a test for emotional intelligence.

1990   **Carolyn Saarni**, a developmental psychologist who specialises in emotional development, spoke about her work on 'emotional competency'. This focused on how children learn to accurately express, understand, and regulate emotions in their interactions with peers, parents and siblings. She published further papers in 1997 and 1999.

1994   **R. Michael Bagby**, **James Parker** and **Graeme Taylor** conducted research on alexithymia which lead to the creation of the Toronto Alexithymia Scale – a measure of the condition which was an improvement on Sifneos' earlier measure.

1995   **Mayer**, **Salovey** and **Caruso** begin work on their test of emotional intelligence. They had heard that a new book on the topic was about to be published which could help them to 'get the word out'.

1995   **Daniel Goleman**'s *Emotional Intelligence* was published. It has now sold over five million copies. Practitioners in the field heard that the working titles of the book were 'Socio-emotional Learning' and 'Emotional Literacy'. Even Goleman's publisher underestimated the impact that this book would have. In the same year, an article appeared in *Time* magazine asking the question 'What's your EQ?' The article stated 'It's not your IQ. It's not even a number. But EQ may be the best predictor of success in life, redefining what it means to be smart.'[xxii] This was to be one of hundreds of newspaper and magazine articles around the world which have popularised the concept.

1996   Dr. **Reuven Bar-On** presented his measure of EQ, the Emotional Quotient Inventory, to the American Psychological Association in Toronto. There was widespread media coverage of his work in North America. Bar-On worked with a Toronto-based test publisher, Multi-Health Systems, to collect more data and refine his instrument. This created the first scientific instrument to measure emotional intelligence, the Bar-On EQ-i, which was published in 1997.

1997   Drs. **John Mayer** and **Peter Salovey** published their revised definition of emotional intelligence and their work on their ability measure of emotional intelligence, the Multifactor Emotional Intelligence Scale (MEIS). In their seminal 1997 paper, they used the following definition: 'Emotional intelligence involves the ability to perceive accurately, appraise, and express emotion; the ability to access and/or generate feelings when they facilitate thought; the ability to understand emotion and emotional knowledge; and the ability to regulate emotions to promote emotional and intellectual growth.'[xxiii]

1998   **Daniel Goleman**'s book *Working with Emotional Intelligence* was published. Much interest in Goleman's first book had come from the corporate world and his second book outlined a set of twenty-five competences for leaders. This book was a bestseller in the business book list. In the same year, the consulting firm that Goleman is associated with, Hay McBer, published a '360-degree' measure of emotional intelligence for people in business – the Emotional Competency Inventory (ECI).

Since 1998, a proliferation of different models, theories, tests and books have emerged. Attention-grabbing headlines have appeared in newspapers, business magazines, airline magazines, and women's magazines all over the world.

Quick Quiz No. 1

1. Which two people coined the term emotional intelligence?

Answer: _____

2. What does alexithymia mean?

Answer: _____

3. Who coined the term EQ?

Answer: _____

4. Who is credited as doing the earliest work on what is now known as emotional intelligence and in which year did he publicise his work?

Answer: _____

5. What are the gender differences in emotional intelligence?

Answer: _____

6. Can emotional intelligence be improved?

Answer: _____

7. Would you expect someone who is 45 years old to be **more** or **less** emotionally intelligent than someone who is 23?

Answer: _____

8. In your own words, what is emotional intelligence?

Answer: _____

9. Is there any hard science that underpins emotional intelligence?

Answer: _____

10. Who did the most to popularise the concept of emotional intelligence?

Answer: _____

Once you have checked your answers, we'll move onto the under-pinning science in Chapter 2.

'Remember, life is not what happens to you
but what you make of what happens to you.
Everyone dies, but not everyone fully lives.
Too many people are having "near life experiences".'
Anonymous

Chapter 2

The Underpinning Science

This chapter covers:

- An explanation of the words 'emotions' and 'intelligence'
- An overview of the brain and the 'location' of emotions
- Recent research findings on the links between emotion and health.

Having reviewed the literature on emotional intelligence, I have discovered that there is no one source that brings together all of the essential facts of the underpinning science of emotional intelligence. One of the reasons for this is that the underpinning science is located in many different fields.[1]

In the last two years, we have doubled our knowledge of neural science and there have been breakthroughs in our knowledge of what emotions are, the connection between the brain and the heart and the role of positive emotions in well-being and personal productivity. Whilst much of this knowledge is in the hands of key researchers and institutes and a few recent excellent books,[i] this chapter aims to summarise important developments in the last decade. Please refer to the references and bibliography for the in-depth scientific references.

Let's start by defining the words 'emotion' and 'intelligence'.

Emotions Defined

Leeper (1948) described emotions as:

"primary motivating forces; they are processes which arouse, sustain and direct activity."[ii]

Whilst there are a number of alternative views on emotions[iii] (see Appendix 1 for a comprehensive list of comments about emotions and feelings), Leeper's simple definition sums up the essentials:

Primary motivating forces – emotions are physical sensations that drive us to act. In fact the word 'emotion' comes from the Latin verb 'emovare' meaning to move. We always have **emotions** – if we are fully functioning and well – they are just as natural as breathing. They are the **vehicle** by which body and mind communicate. They are constantly changing and moving – **e-motion**. Part

---

[1] Including general medicine, physics, neurology, neuroanatomy, neuroradiology, endocrinology, cardiology, psychiatry, neurophysiology, neuropsychology, immunology and biology!

of emotional intelligence involves controlling these forces, especially when they are likely to get us into trouble (see section on the amygdala – chapter 2).

Processes – Candace Pert has studied the physical composition of emotions and has found that they are the result of a number of chemical processes. Emotions are represented in the physical form of peptides – they are made up of "neuropeptides and receptors, the biochemicals of emotion, … the messengers carrying information to link the major systems of the body into one unit that we can call the body-mind. We can no longer think of the emotions as having less validity than physical, material substance, but instead must see them as cellular signals that are involved in the process of translating information into physical reality, literally transforming mind into matter. Emotions are at the nexus between matter and mind, going back and forth between the two and influencing both."[iv] In other words, our thinking and our health are connected. What connects them are our emotions.

Arouse, Sustain and Direct activity – One way of thinking about emotions is to consider them as 'messengers' carrying information that we need in order to make decisions and survive. They are often **automatic** responses to internal and external happenings based on past experiences. They are instinctive, and often based on our whole databank of emotional memories. What this means is that when we experience something, 'at best we feel and think at the same time, in most situations, we feel before we think'.[v] Research done by Rita Carter shows that when neural pathways in the brain are lit up during the experience of a disgusting event, these are exactly the same pathways that are lit up when the experience is recalled.[vi] In other words the memory of something happening created and sustained an identical set of neural pathways in the brain as the actual experience of it.

This is important when we are interacting with people. If, for example, you are spending a week with your mother-in-law and want it to be pleasant, it is best to remember positive interactions where you experienced heartfelt emotions like love and appreciation. It will allow you to emotionally react to her in a loving way. If you are about to go for an interview, remembering a positive experience of being successful at an interview will start to create the same neural activity in the brain as the experience actually happening. All interview questions will be easy to interpret when we set the proper emotional stage!

Now you can begin to realise the influence our emotions have on our lives. Our emotions are a powerful **untapped resource** that we are only just waking up to. For too long, we have thought that emotions 'get in the way' – but they get in the way only when we do not know how to understand them, manage them, and make sense of what is happening. The power lies in understanding and regulating our thoughts, feelings and actions. This creates the most robust **wiring** in the brain. However, most of us are not 'in touch with our feelings'. Much of our early life reinforced the need *not* to show our emotions – so many people are cut off from a major source of information. In short, emotions compel us to act, react, withdraw. They inform our thoughts and actions and impact everything we do.

Intelligence Defined

According to Drs. John Mayer and Peter Salovey,[vii] emotional intelligence as they define it has the same characteristics as other intelligences, namely:

1. There are right and wrong answers to the questions and scenarios included in the emotional intelligence test.
2. The abilities forming the intelligence have some relation to each other – they rise and fall as a group but they are also distinct of other intelligences.
3. The absolute ability level rises with age and experience. In other words you would expect a 5 year old to be more emotionally intelligent than a 2 year old.

Only one of the current models of emotional intelligence meets all three of these criteria (see chapter 3 on schools of emotional intelligence). Emotional intelligence as defined by Mayer, Salovey &

Caruso is the only true, separate 'intelligence'. The other models of emotional intelligence are more accurately referred to as a set of capabilities, desirable characteristics or skills that make a difference in life.

Now that we have considered definitions of 'emotion' and 'intelligence', let's move now to the brain and the physical qualities of emotions.

Overview of the Brain and the Location of Emotions

The brain and the underpinning science of emotional intelligence is a complex subject. What is presented here is a simplification designed to highlight the key points and principles. Apologies in advance to all neurophysiologists reading this work!

The limbic system (or emotional brain) plays a major part in our experience and expression of emotions.[2] This part of the brain initially evolved for feeding, mating and defence of territory. This is still the part of the brain we use for evaluating what is happening and generating appropriate physiological reactions in the body

---

[2] It was once assumed that the thinking brain grew out of the emotional regions – the Triune Brain Theory – however, this idea that the brainstem evolved first, then the limbic, then the cognitive, has now been disproved. This important breakthrough came in 1937 when James Papex, a neuroanatomy professor at Cornell University, described a circuit and suggested that it might constitute the neural substrate for emotion, thus introducing the idea of a circuit rather than a center. He suggested that blockage of information flow at any point along this circuit would cause disorder of emotions. Now known as the Papez circuit, this model described the flow of information from the hippocampal formation to the thalamus, then to the cingulated gyrus and back again to the hippocampal formation. This was later elaborated on by Paul Maclean, chief of the laboratory for brain evolution and behaviour at the National Institute for Mental Health in Bethesda, Maryland. In the 1950s, Maclean introduced the concept of the 'limbic system'. He also originated the Triune Brain model, which delineated three functional brain systems which he believed developed successively in response to evolutionary needs. Although Maclean's theory has had little impact on neurobiology, it has become popular in the lay press and with psychotherapists. However, it should be noted that extensive work in comparative neurobiology unequivocally contradicts the evolutionary aspects of his theory (source: Dr. Alan Watkins).

(e.g. regulating temperature, sweat, thirst, hunger pangs). Let's look at the limbic system in this simplified diagram (please note: this is not drawn to scale):

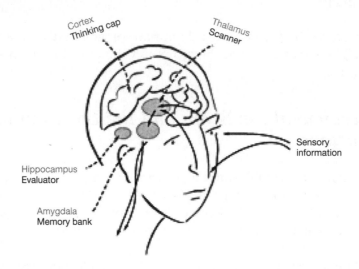

All information that enters the brain comes into the **Thalamus** before being distributed to other parts of the brain – labelled here as the **SCANNER** as it constantly scans the environment for information.

When the **SCANNER** recognises patterns of experience that led to previous emotional reactions, it relays this information to the **hippocampus** within the emotional center of the brain. This is labelled here as **EVALUATOR** because it has an 'evaluative' function to assess context, comparing current information with what has been seen before. The amygdala labelled here **MEMORY BANK** determines the emotional significance of events and compares the threat with past events; it has a role in storing emotional memories. If there is a positive match with earlier memories, it is the **MEMORY BANK** which gets involved to initiate a fight or flight response. (Is it a threat? Do I run away? Or do I stay and fight?) If there is no match, the information is relayed to the Cortex the **THINKING CAP** responsible for rational processes. The Amygdala is our **MEMORY BANK** where we store all our emotional memories from childhood and throughout our life. When we experience disappointment or sadness, that memory gets stored away – equally, every time someone shouts at us as children, that memory is kept in our emotions bank. When the **MEMORY BANK** finds emotional content in a particular experience, it files it away in its memory and it triggers a physiological response to protect us. So for instance, if it perceives threat or fear based on the comparison with past experience, it creates the **fight or flight response** (e.g. speeds up heart rate, increases blood pressure etc.). Of course, this process happens in a flash. When we experience strong emotions, the fight-flight response that is designed to protect us can impair our ability to hear, think and speak with clarity. Have you ever had the experience of going to speak in front of an audience and your whole body clams up?

An example of this is when you are on a plane and you are about to touch down at your destination. During the descent the plane drops several feet and your stomach gets left in the air. The **MEMORY BANK (amygdala)** sends a signal to the rest of body to 'get ready to take action' – the **THINKING CAP** is still mulling over whether there is any real danger. After a few more seconds of this experience, the **MEMORY BANK** decides whether or not to be scared. This decision will be based on all previous memories and information stored in this bank of memories. The **MEMORY BANK** will trigger a physiological response to speed up both blood pressure and heart rate to prepare itself for an emergency landing.

Problems occur because the **EVALUATOR** is quite imprecise in its matching of current situations to memories. So if the situation that presents itself is 'boss arrives to have a chat with me' it could well match it with a similar but not identical experience of 'feeling scared in the dark as a child'. This is what creates the **hard wiring** in our brains – where our reactions based on 'old information' are almost automatic. We can trigger strong emotions from a relatively minor event.

Although the structures just described in the limbic system interconnect, research has shown that it is the **MEMORY BANK** and the **EVALUATOR** which seem to be the main areas of the brain involved in the emotions.

Let's focus on a feeling of happiness – perhaps a feeling of happiness based on something we have seen – which is routed to the **SCANNER** keeping constant watch on what is happening. The

SCANNER directs the impulse to the **THINKING CAP** for processing so that the cortex can think about the impulse and make sense of it. 'Aha,' it says, 'this is the person I love! I am really looking forward to our evening together. I feel quite excited!' That signal is then sent to the **MEMORY BANK** where a flood of peptides and hormones are released to create emotion and action.[viii]

Let's look at what happens in the brain when you experience strong negative emotion. (Or strong anything, for that matter.)[ix]

The problem occurs when we experience strong emotion and the information does not go to the **THINKING CAP** – it goes straight to the **MEMORY BANK**. For instance, if you are walking down a street one night and you are scared, it is the **MEMORY BANK** that will trigger the reactions in your body – the fear turns on the sympathetic nervous system which produces an increase in body temperature, blood pressure and the blood gets moved to our legs (say, away from our digestive system dealing with our last meal) so that we can run away. Daniel Goleman in his books refers to this as an 'amygdala hijack'. Joseph Ledoux, a neuroscientist at the New York University Center for Neuroscience refers to the **MEMORY BANK** (the Amygdala) as the 'hub of fear'[x] – 'what its doing is sitting around waiting to detect danger. If nothing particular is going on, cells in the amygdala literally just sit there doing nothing. In some areas of the brain the cells could be firing away all the time, but in the amygdala, the cells are very, very silent, quiet. They just don't do anything unless there's something important. And once something important happens, they just start firing away, popping along.'[xi]

Recent Research Findings

As mentioned earlier, there have been great developments in our understanding of the neural pathways in the brain and in our understanding of the power of the human heart in recent years. Though science and emotion were two topics rarely paired together, there is a growing body of researchers around the world investigating new developments that have the power to change what we will see in future included on school curricula, in workplace training programmes and in community projects.

The following 'round up' of current research gives you an overview of some interesting developments.

- **There is a difference in the levels of activity in the MEMORY BANK (Amygdala) depending on whether negative or positive emotion is experienced.**
  Richard Davidson, professor of psychology and psychiatry at the University of Wisconsin who directs the Brain Imaging Laboratory has compared brain scans of a 'positive resilient' group with a group he describes as 'negative and vulnerable'. He has found that there is more activity in the negative group in the amygdala, which is associated with negative emotion and stress.[xii] Jerome Kagan at Harvard University is studying the different brain chemistries of children and he has found a similar difference in children much younger in life showing more activity in a certain part of the brain.[xiii]

- **False signs of emotion can be detected**
  Antonio Damasio heads the Department of Neurology at the University of Iowa College of Medicine – one of the world's leading authorities on emotions and the brain. He has found that false signs of emotion do not convince others, "if you're trying to smile just because you're polite. If you're trying to indicate happiness when, in fact, you don't feel it, you're going to have to exert a voluntary control and you're going to try to make believe you are happy. And when that happens, the machinery that you use to produce that smile, or to produce laughter, is not the one that the brain normally uses in the involuntary, natural condition. And as a result, your smile or your laughter may sound false."[xiv]

- **The heart has its own brain and its own nervous system**
  John Andrew Armour, a famous neurocardiologist from Dalhousie University, Halifax, Nova Scotia, has discovered that the heart has its own brain and nervous systems (just like the brain). In 1991 research started to focus attention on the heart as a powerhouse of energy and intelligence.[xv] In fact,

Armour created the field 'neurocardiology' and wrote a book by the same name. Through this emerging science of neurocardiology it has been learned that this "heart brain" has highly sophisticated computational abilities and affects both heart and brain function. No longer can we think that our 'intelligence' resides in our brain. While many researchers focused on the brain to find mood-and performance-altering neurochemicals such as nor epinephrine and dopamine, researchers from the field of neurocardiology discovered these being quietly produced within the heart as well, along with hormones such as ANF, known as the balancing hormone, and oxytocin, known as the bonding hormone.[xvi] They learned that these chemicals in the heart in turn affect brain processing and virtually every other organ in the body.[xvii]

- **Emotions exist as chemical reactions**
  Candace Pert has conducted studies into the molecular make-up of emotions and has confirmed that emotions have a chemical signature.

- **Whole body representation of emotions**
  Emotions involve a number of different organs and systems in the body, including the heart, brain, autonomic nervous system, hormonal system and sensory organs, and therefore all of these influence thoughts and behaviour. I have suspected this for a long time – a number of years ago, my osteopath told me that he had completed several manipulations on people who he suspects had had long buried emotional memories released – a painful process that often left them gasping on the adjustment table. I think that it is really important for us to go beyond the 'brain' and realise that we have a 'whole body response' to our emotions, which affects our health and well-being either positively, in the case of positive emotions, or negatively, in the case of disruptive emotions like fear and anger. It is no longer right therefore to dismiss emotions from our day-to-day experience of life – they are linked to our whole experience of the world.

- **All decisions involve the emotions**
  The world famous neuroscientist, Antonio Damasio has been researching the role of emotions in decision making. His

seminal work has been with patients who have brain lesions in the emotional center of the brain. Through years of different studies, he has confirmed that patients who have received a blow to the pathway between their **THINKING CAP** and the **MEMORY BANK** are unable to make a decision. So, for instance, when he asked a patient for the time, they could accurately answer him. But when he asked a question that involved a choice – for instance, 'when would you like your next appointment?' or any question that has a notion of personal opinion or preference, patients were typically unable to make a decision.[xviii] This blew out the notion that thoughts and feelings are separate – well, in reality they are, until we have to make a decision. 100% of our decisions therefore involve our feelings. Emotions are a **natural** and **normal** part of reasoning and decision-making. It is important for us therefore to recognise and acknowledge the power of the emotions in our decisions.

- **Positive emotion influences our perception of time**
  Kimberley Babb of the University of California presented a study at the American Psychological Society in December 2000 on the effect of emotions on our perception of time. She used film clips to induce one of 4 emotional states in 128 students – happiness, sadness, fear and neutral – and she then set them to a task. They were asked to guess when a minute had elapsed. The students who were neutral or happy were able to guess accurately the passage of 1 minute, but the students who were fearful or sad overestimated the time – so our emotional state affects our perception of time.[xix] Have you ever had the experience of time flying by when you are having fun? I remember that when I saw the film *Reservoir Dogs* which was under 2 hours long, I ended up walking out of it half way as I didn't enjoy the film. But the following week, I saw the James Bond film *Golden Eye*, a longer film which seemed to be over in a flash – at the end of it, I could have sat through the whole film again.

- **Heart/brain connection**
  Doc Childre has been researching stress as a major inhibitor of perception and performance. In 1991, he founded the Institute of HeartMath which has brought together researchers who have studied the power of the heart as a source of power for managing personal demands and pressures.

Through a number of studies, it has been found that the heart affects the brain's performance in the following ways:

1. The heart produces mood enhancing and performance-altering hormones.
2. The heart produces an electro-magnetic signal that reaches every cell in the body, including the brain, and it communicates mechanically through pressure waves conducted along blood vessels.
3. Beat to beat changes in heart rate (Heart Rate Variability or HRV) have a pattern (as measured by an electro cardiogram) that is different when we are stressed compared to when we are in balance. These patterns influence in turn the brain's ability to think and process information. Our emotional state therefore causes measurable changes in the brain's ability to think and process information.
4. In other words our heart influences our brain – when the electrical patterns of the brain 'entrain' or synchronise with the rhythmic patterns of the heart, we operate with greater coherence and therefore can think quicker and act smarter.

Researchers at the Institute of HeartMath have discovered that people in negative emotional states perform less well and are less productive compared to people in positive emotional states, who have more clarity and better quality of thinking in their lives. The work of the Institute of HeartMath is summarised in a book published two years ago *The HeartMath Solution*. In this book, Doc Childre outlines the research and the techniques that are contained within the HeartMath system for achieving better personal productivity. If the techniques were implemented on a grand scale, the difference to our health would be significant.[3] The key points about the HeartMath system are listed below:

1. It is the heart that is the key to bringing harmony to the mind and body.

---

[3] In one case study in a well-known petrochemical company, a group of people were taught the techniques of the HeartMath system and a range of data was collected before the training, 6 weeks after and 6 months after a one-day workshop. The systolic and diastolic blood pressure of senior people (a useful measure of overall health) reduced by 9 mm Hg and 5mm Hg respectively after only 6 weeks. The replication of this result over a whole population could reduce the incidence of stroke by 60%. Reference: Hunter Kane Resource Management case study 10.

2. It is therefore the heart that can influence our thinking, physiology, feelings and behaviour.

3. The signal received by the brain from the heart is the most powerful signal in the body. The electro-magnetic field produced by the heart is five thousand times greater in strength than the field generated by the brain and can be detected and measured several feet away from the body, in all directions.[xx] The heart produces 40 to 60 times the electrical amplitude generated by the activity of the brain, and this electrical signal can be measured anywhere on the body.[xxi]

4. The heart communicates with the other 'systems' in the body, for instance the immune system. Each system has its own set of electrical impulses, and cells throughout our body feel the waves of pressure generated by the heart. Because the heart is the most powerful organ, the signal generated by the heart has the power to influence the rest of the body.

5. The Institute of HeartMath has found that a feeling of positive emotion has the power to send a coherent signal from the heart to the brain, thus freeing up our thinking and our clarity of perception. There is a piece of software that the Institute has developed for individual use[xxii] so that you can measure the coherence of the heart signal that you generate.[xxiii] Incoherence or chaos promotes cortical inhibition, or brain shut down – quite literally, your 'cortex' or thinking cap is affected – many of us experience this when we do things in a rush, make hasty decisions, say things under stress that we later regret, or feel 'out of sorts' when we cannot get our physical co-ordination right.

6. The Institute of HeartMath has created a number of techniques which can be used to achieve more internal coherence[xxiv] and greater connection between heart and brain.

7. This includes the practice of generating positive emotions like care and appreciation, using positive emotion when facing difficult situations (in order to free up your thinking) and the use of specially designed music to help heighten mental and emotional balance[xxv] – this music has proven to increase the concentration of antibodies in the saliva, our first line of defence against flu and colds[xxvi] (see Appendix 6 for details of this and other HeartMath products). The contact information for HeartMath can be found in Appendix 4.

So in summary, according to HeartMath research, the heart has the power to bring our physical systems into balance. It is the heart and not the brain that is the 'powerhouse' in the body, so learning how to use the power of our heart could also be useful for helping us to cope with stress and change. As Bruce Cryer commented in a recent article: 'it has now become clear that intelligence is distributed throughout the human system — not just localised in the brain — and that the heart is an intelligent system profoundly affecting brain processing.'[xxvii]

- **Hormonal system**
  Finally, scientific studies have proved that the hormonal system is partly regulated by the brain's emotional circuits. A key daily rhythm is our daily variation in **cortisol** and **DHEA** levels. In recent years a number of researchers have proposed the DHEA/cortisol ratio to be a good biological marker of stress and aging. Each of these hormones is explained below.

CORTISOL
1. Cortisol is one of the most important molecules in the body, as it is involved in a variety of physiological and psychological processes.
2. Our cortisol level usually peaks between 07:00 AM and 08:00 AM and then declines to a low between 23:00 and midnight.
3. Cortisol has a central role in metabolism, health, memory, and learning as well as in the body's ability to be immune to disease. In balanced amounts, cortisol is essential for the healthy functioning of our bodies
4. Anyone who is under chronic stress would have high levels of cortisol. Cortisol is sometimes referred to as the 'stress hormone'. because it is secreted in excessive amounts when people are under stress.

DHEA
1. DHEA is the body's natural antidote to cortisol; it is known as the 'anti-aging hormone' and is the precursor to the human sex hormones oestrogen and testosterone.
2. Its many and varied physiological effects include enhancement of the immune system, stimulation of bone deposition, lowering cholesterol levels and building muscle mass.

CORTISOL/DHEA Levels

1. The body is not able to produce both DHEA and cortisol at the same time so often with high levels of cortisol, the production of DHEA will be restricted.
2. When individuals are under prolonged stress, cortisol levels continue to rise while DHEA levels decrease significantly – this creates an imbalance, the effects of which can be severe and may include elevated blood sugar levels, increased bone loss, compromised immune function, decreased skin repair and regeneration, increased fat accumulation and brain cell destruction.[xxviii] When cortisol levels rise too high, it can be extremely dangerous to us. A recent study reported in the September issues of Psychosomatic Medicine suggested that slender women who have higher levels of cortisol (the stress hormone) tend to have more abdominal fat which is known to increase the risk of several disorders, including heart disease and diabetes.[xxix]
3. DHEA has been found to be deficient in individuals with many major diseases and conditions, including obesity, diabetes, hypertension, cancer, Alzheimer's, immune deficiency, coronary artery disease and various autoimmune disorders.

Reducing cortisol and increasing DHEA

Being aware of this hormonal balance gives us new information to focus on, in staying healthy and happy. So what is the remedy to decreased DHEA?

1. Levels of DHEA can be increased naturally through positive emotion. DHEA is thought to be a natural anti-depressant; it can improve memory, slow down the ageing process and prevent cancer.
2. Replacing cortisol with DHEA, through activating positive emotion, can reduce cortisol levels. Feeling happy is actually good for your health and this is what explains why some people often look younger than their years (lots of DHEA) or have aged too quickly (high levels of cortisol).
3. Natural ways to increase DHEA can be learned through the use of HeartMath techniques.

- **Physical touch, being in love and optimism is good**
  In a fascinating study done by Candace Pert with monkeys to determine maternal influence, a group of monkey babies were raised by fake monkey mothers, a wire-and-cloth structure with milk bottles instead of breasts. The babies were fed but not touched, cuddled, or held. They soon developed all the signs of trauma and depression through the creation of high levels of steroids in the body, which are linked to depression. Fortunately they were cured and their stress symptoms were reversed when researchers brought in monkey hug therapists! The hugging monkeys helped to break the state of trauma, by sending the message to the body 'No more steroids needed' through their hugging. The chronically elevated levels of steroids came down.[xxx] In another study on physical touch conducted by the Institute of HeartMath, researchers found that when people touch or are in proximity, one person's heartbeat signal is registered in the other person's brain-waves.[xxxi] Signal averaging techniques were used to show that one's electrocardiogram (ECG) signal is registered in another person's electroencephalogram (EEG) and elsewhere on the other person's body. While researchers found that this signal was strongest when people were in contact (in this study they were holding hands), it was still detectable when subjects were close but not touching and in some cases, the interaction could be detected even when the subjects were four feet apart.

In another study by Dr. Andrea Bartels at University College London, researchers have been able to identify the parts of the brain that are responsible for deep, romantic feelings. They gathered together 17 people who reported that they were truly madly in love and recorded brain scans while they were shown photographs of their loved ones. There was an increase in the blood flow in 4 regions of the emotional brain and reduced activity in the neocortex.[xxxii]

In a recent study by the Mayo Clinic in Rochester, Minnesota, the medical histories of 839 people were tracked over 30 years – they had all completed a standard personality test between 1962 and 1965 measuring their optimism (124 optimists, 197 pessimists and 518 in between). Their death rates were compared and every 10-point increase in pessimism was asso-ciated with a 19% increase in death rate![xxxiii] Staying optimistic means that we are likely to live longer. There are similar studies which have been done recently on the role of optimism in reducing adverse outcomes in high-risk pregnancies, helping HIV-positive men maintain health, speeding recovery from heart bypass surgery and as part of the treatment for teenagers who take drugs.[xxxiv]

With all of the messages we send out to keep healthy, the most important is to hug and love each other and stay positive!

- **Gender differences**
  In a recent study at the Indiana University School of Medicine, 10 men and women were studied while they listened to a John Grisham thriller. MRI scans (which measure high speed changes in neural blood flow) were used to compare activity in their brains. Researchers found that women use their whole brain whereas men used half of their brain.[xxxv]

Now that we have discussed the underpinning science to emotional intelligence, the next chapter will focus on the different schools of emotional intelligence.

Quick Quiz No. 2

1. Which hormone is most associated with positive emotion?

Answer: _____

2. Which hormone is most associated with negative emotion?

Answer: _____

3. Which is the most powerful organ in the body electrically and electro-magnetically?

Answer: _____

4. What does the original Latin translation of the word 'emotion' mean?

Answer: _____

5. Which part of the brain is responsible for housing emotional memories?

Answer: _____

6. Which part of the brain is responsible for thinking?

Answer: _____

7. What is the name of the institute in California, which has researched the health benefits of using the heart to help increase the power of the brain and the clarity of our thinking?

Answer: _____

8. What is the name of the female researcher who has researched the molecular make-up of emotions?

Answer: _____

'The antidote to exhaustion is not rest.
The antidote to exhaustion is wholeheartedness.'
David Whyte, Poet
— September 1999, Linkage conference on
Emotional intelligence, Chicago

Chapter 3

The 'Schools' of Emotional Intelligence

This chapter covers:

- The three main schools that adopt a 'whole-life' approach to the measurement of emotional intelligence
- How to choose a measure of emotional intelligence
- Summary of the most useful measures currently available.

Many people around the world are doing good work on emotional intelligence, researching definitions and creating tests that help to measure Ei. There is a growing volume of academic papers written on the subject, and a rapidly evolving student population who are choosing emotional intelligence as their specialist area of study. Within the space of just three months, I have been in contact with students researching emotional intelligence and trauma, emotional intelligence and work culture, and emotional intelligence in call centres.

When you are new to the concept, how do you go about measuring your own emotional intelligence? Some of the available measures are certainly better researched and more useful than others. It is generally accepted that it takes a minimum of five years to create a valid and reliable measure of emotional intelligence, so I would be sceptical of anything that has been created more recently than this.

At a conference in May 2000 at the Commonwealth Institute in London, John Mayer (who – with Peter Salovey – had first coined the term 'emotional intelligence') entitled one of his papers, 'Which Emotional Intelligence?' He proposed that the debate over the next few years would focus on 'Which emotional intelligence are you talking about?'[i] This question is the subject of much current debate in the field and this chapter aims to clarify the situation. It looks at the different measures and their underlying definitions of emotional intelligence, so that after reading it you will be able to make a considered choice on how to measure your own emotional intelligence.

The chapter focuses on the three schools that measure emotional intelligence as a whole-life concept. I have found in my own practice that these measures are all useful. These three schools don't, however, represent the full range of the available instruments and measures. If you want to explore a wider set of instruments, the lists provided in Appendices 3, 4 and 5 will give you an easy starting point.

There are also three business schools of emotional intelligence that are primarily focused on emotional intelligence in the workplace. Descriptions of these can be found in Appendix 3.

In presenting this summary, I would like to stress that whilst I set out to be objective in my descriptions, they are based on my own experiences and are therefore subjective. My opinion of the available instruments has been shaped by the particular applications that I work with and the issues I have faced when answering concerns and questions from individuals on the measurement of their emotional intelligence. The main applications I currently work with are training and development, recruitment, executive coaching, programmes for teams and programmes in the education sector measuring children's and teachers' levels of emotional intelligence.

In a relatively new field, details of the available instruments can change over time, so I suggest you use the contact details listed in Appendix 2 to check the up-to-date details by contacting the appropriate test publishers.

'Whole Life' Schools of Emotional Intelligence

This section covers these three 'schools' and their measures:

1. Dr. Reuven Bar-On and the Bar-On Emotional Quotient Inventory (EQ-i)
2. Drs. John Mayer, Peter Salovey and David Caruso and the Multifactor Emotional Intelligence Scale (MEIS)
3. The Institute for Health and Human Potential (IHHP) and the EI-360.

Each school is introduced in the following way:

- Who is behind each 'school'
- My view as a practitioner on the benefits and downsides of each measure
- An overview of the school's definition and measure of emotional intelligence.[ii]

1. The Bar-On Emotional Quotient Inventory (EQ-i)

Who is Behind the Bar-On EQ-i?

Dr. Reuven Bar-On is the clinical psychologist and meticulous clinician/researcher who has spent over nineteen years researching EQ and developing the EQ-i. He will be co-directing the Emotional Intelligence Research Laboratory at Trent University in Canada. He coined the expression Emotional Quotient (EQ) in 1985. In 1995, he met Dr. Steve Stein (Chief Executive Officer of Multi-Health Systems, a major test publisher in Toronto) at a dinner in Israel, where Stein was making a presentation. When Stein heard about the 'quiet research work' that Bar-On had been doing since 1980 on something called 'Emotional Quotient', he suggested that Bar-On send the materials to him in Toronto. Since 1995, Bar-On has been working alongside Multi-Health Systems to refine the measure of emotional intelligence, broaden its research base to cover North America and publish a family of products so that the inventory can reach a large number of researchers and clinicians. The Bar-On Emotional Quotient Inventory was officially launched in 1997 in North America by Multi-Health Systems and has since been published in fourteen languages.[iii] Research data has been collected in twenty-two languages[iv] across a range of professions and this has confirmed the inventory's reliability as a measure of emotional intelligence.

Definition of Emotional Intelligence

Dr. Reuven Bar-On defines emotional intelligence as an 'array of emotional, personal and social abilities which influence one's overall ability to cope effectively with environmental demands and pressures.'[v] In other words, it includes skills that we need in order to cope with day-to-day life.

What Does the Bar-On EQ-i Measure, and How?

In short, the Bar-On EQ-i measures your Emotional Quotient. It uses a questionnaire containing 133 items that you are asked to score on a scale of 1 to 5, where 1 is 'very seldom or not true of me' and 5 is 'very often true of me or true of me'. The five main components measured by the inventory are:

- *intrapersonal* – the ability to be aware of, understand and express one's emotions
- *interpersonal* – the ability to be aware of, understand and accept the feelings of others as well as to relate well with them
- *adaptability* – the ability to adapt your feelings, thoughts and behaviour to changing conditions and situations and to manage change in general
- *stress management* – the ability to manage emotions so that they work for you and not against you
- *general mood* – the ability to motivate yourself.[vi]

Appendix 2 contains a fuller description of what is contained within each of these aspects of EQ.

Benefits of the Bar-On EQ-i

1. A solid and extensive research base underpins this instrument, with close to two decades of research studies – far more than any other emotional intelligence measurement tool currently available. To ensure that the instrument is valid cross-culturally, research studies have been completed in Argentina, Canada, Chile, Germany, Great Britain, India, Israel, Mexico, Nigeria, the Philippines, South Africa, Sweden and the United States.[vii]
2. The underpinning research base has created a set of impressive 'norms'.[viii] These help to ensure that the test is valid and reliable. It is suitable for use in recruitment – in fact, is the only available measure of emotional intelligence that has the validity and norms to make its use for recruitment possible.
3. It is the only measure of emotional intelligence that actually measures 'EQ' which is so often quoted in articles.
4. Some report formats give you the option of calculating the numeric values of EQ (anything between 85 and 115 is average or effective functioning) so it is easy to pick out the individual's areas of weakness. Some people like to know how 'good' their EQ is.

5. This is a simple model of emotional intelligence that everyone seems to be able to relate to, at all levels, and in all contexts of work and personal life.
6. There is now a family of Bar-On EQ-i products available, including the youth version (for children aged six to eighteen), and software for scoring questionnaires and printing reports. A number of products are under development, including a 'multi-rater' version (called the EQ.360) and a semi-structured interview (EQ interview) for use in recruitment situations.
7. There are four validity indicators that make the test hard to fake.[ix]
8. It is relatively easy to administer, score and interpret. It takes approximately thirty minutes to complete.
9. There are four different report formats – a five-page individual summary report, an eleven-page resource report, a seventeen-page development report and a group report.
10. Scores can be compared to people of the same age and gender or to the general population. Again, it is the only instrument that has extensive data that make such comparisons possible.
11. Many people have described the results as 'life-changing' and 'insightful' during sessions where I have provided individual feedback on the results.

Downsides of the Bar-On EQ-i

1. Some psychologists state that self-estimates have low accuracy.[x]
2. Individuals who administer the questionnaire must be trained and certified by the test publisher or a company licensed by the test publisher (see Appendices 2, 3 and 4), and there are selection criteria for being able to train as a user. This restricts use of the test.
3. Some academics claim that this measure of emotional intelligence covers many aspects already covered by other measures of personality.

A Final Word

An excellent research base underpins this instrument. It is very easy to understand, complete and make sense of the results. Is powerful for starting a conversation about "what is really going on" in a person's life.

2 *The Multifactor Emotional Intelligence Scale (MEIS)*

Who is Behind the Multifactor Emotional Intelligence Scale?

Drs. John Mayer and Peter Salovey are the originators of the term 'emotional intelligence'.[xi] Mayer is Professor of Psychology at the University of New Hampshire, and Peter is Chairperson, Department of Psychology at Yale University. They teamed up with David Caruso to produce the first ability measure of emotional intelligence, called the Multifactor Emotional Intelligence Scale (or MEIS), which measures your ability to identify, use, understand and manage emotion. The MEIS has the 'look' of a written test paper, where some answers are more 'right' than others. Sample items are included in Chapter 4, where you will have the opportunity to measure your own emotional intelligence by the MEIS. The MEIS is distributed by Charles J. Wolfe Associates (see Appendix 2).

Definition of Emotional Intelligence

Mayer, Salovey and Caruso define emotional intelligence as: 'the ability to perceive, appraise, and express emotion accurately and adaptively; the ability to understand emotion and emotional knowledge; the ability to access and/or generate feelings when they facilitate thought; and the ability to regulate emotions in ways that assist thought.'[xii] In other words, it is about being able to identify emotions in others and yourself; being able to relate to other people by reading their emotions and your own, and managing emotions in the heat of day-to-day situations.

What does the MEIS Measure, and How?

The MEIS contains 122 questions, grouped within six different sub-tests contained within a nine-page reusable test booklet. The sub-tests are in different formats, each of which requires the test taker to score from 1 to 5 to indicate the extent to which a particular emotion is present, from 'definitely not present' to 'definitely present'.

For example, one sub-test includes a description of a situation seen from two different people's perspectives and you are asked to rate the presence of particular emotions from each person's perspective; in another sub-test, you are asked to review different emotions and accurately name them as the emotion gets more intense.

Benefits of the MEIS

1. It defines a special and unique set of four abilities, each of which includes the word 'emotions' – it can therefore offer new insights in how you are dealing with the emotional part of life. It seems to measure something quite distinct from the other available instruments. It is the only measure that meets the criteria for an 'intelligence' (see Chapter 2).
2. It does not involve the 'hassle' of asking other people to assess your emotional intelligence, which can often be a cumbersome and slow process, and which often involves waiting for questionnaires to be returned when disorganised friends and family members have not completed them in time.
3. It is a paper-and-pencil test, so it is easy to use and to score.
4. Results are simple to understand and specific, so development needs can be identified easily.
5. This is a deep model – the four branches give you interesting insights into how you are dealing with the emotional content of life. It deals with how people think, decide, plan and create, and is skills-based.[xiii]
6. Most development areas can be addressed and improved.
7. It is hard to 'fake' as there are answers which are considered 'better' than others. In researching the questionnaire, the 'right' answer was decided through methods of scoring including consensus (a large audience of people were asked

the questions and their answers formed the consensus view) and expert opinion (experts on emotions were asked for their answers to the same questions), and the two are merged to create the scoring system.

8. It does not require trained users to score the test.

Downsides of the MEIS

1. Data does not currently exist to support its use for selection or to predict successful performance at work – so it can only be used for development at this point.
2. The test looks similar to an exam, which can be off-putting for some.
3. There is a generic feedback booklet and score sheet, but at the time of writing a computer-generated report is not yet available. So the whole testing process is relatively low-tech, although a web-enabled version of the next generation of test (called the MSCEIT – Mayer, Salovey, Caruso Emotional Intelligence Test) is currently under development.

A Final Word

A very interesting test to complete. Unique in the field of emotional intelligence.

3. The EI-360

Who is behind it?

The Institute for Health and Human Potential (IHHP) is a North American company specialising in the design and delivery of programmes in emotional intelligence for leaders, managers, sales teams, Olympic and elite athletes. The head of the institute is Dr. Pawliw-Fry, a Performance Coach and Psychologist who has developed unique programmes in emotional intelligence. He and colleagues created their own measure, the EI-360, when they felt that some important factors (e.g. authenticity) were missing from available measures.

Definition of Emotional Intelligence

J.P. Pawliw-Fry defines emotional intelligence as 'the capacity for effectively recognising and managing our own emotions and those of others.'[xiv]

What does the EI-360 Measure, and How?

The EI-360 measures:

- self-awareness
- emotional management
- emotional connection
- personal leadership.

It contains forty-seven statements that you and others are asked to rate on a seven-point scale from 'Not at all' to 'Always' with a 'Don't know' option. So the measurement comprises a self-assessment plus an assessment for completion by up to ten 'raters'– other people, including family, peers, and colleagues. The whole process takes place on the internet. The individual who is being assessed mails the questionnaires to other people to complete on their behalf.

See Appendix 3 for more details.

Benefits of the EI-360

1. It is fully web-enabled so is accessible to anyone.
2. It enables a comparison of perceptions of your emotional intelligence – how emotionally intelligent you perceive yourself to be, compared with other people's perceptions of you.
3. Attractive, user-friendly report, with good mix of words and visuals. One particularly useful feature is that all scores are ranked in order from highest to lowest. (This feature is not part of any other report that I have reviewed.)
4. Has the facility for raters (the term used for 'other people' who provide scores on your emotional intelligence) to be drawn from five possible categories – Manager, Direct Report, Peer,

Family and Key Client. The rater familiarity is taken into account in the weighting of the final results.

5. There is space for each person assessing you to add comments – a full summary of these is provided within the report.

6. The report is divided into groups of different types of raters – e.g. personal life, work life – and you get a score of total 'rater agreement'.

7. There are two open questions at the end, where other people are asked to state the strengths that they hope the person will keep and the development areas for this person to grow. These comments then form part of the full EI-360 report.

8. Applicable for anyone, whether in a leadership role in work or not.

9. Written in universal English, so easy to use across the world.

10. Has a rapidly growing database of norms.

11. There is an optional 'EQ climate snapshot' which provides a reading of the environment directly surrounding the individual having their EQ measured. This helps the individual to understand the environment in which they are living – thus providing some context for their everyday behaviour.

Downsides of the EI-360

1. The instrument only exists in a multi-rater format (i.e. for completion by you and up to ten others) – at the time of writing it isn't possible to use it for self-assessment.

2. There are no 'successful profiles' yet based on this measure, so there is no basis for comparison in order to identify what level of EQ to aim for – this instrument is more useful for comparing *perceptions* of your emotional intelligence.

3. The seven-point scale is unusual and may not sufficiently force the scores in one direction – in my opinion a five-point score or a four-point score usually gives you clearer trends.

A Final Word

Very user-friendly, provides useful information from other people. Interesting measurement device.

Choosing a Measure of Emotional Intelligence

Whilst all the available measures refer to 'emotional intelligence', you will have noticed that the definitions and therefore the method of measurement differ. So it is really important to choose the best measure for you. The questions that follow should help you to make the right choice.

Ask yourself the following questions when choosing a measure:

1. What does this test measure? (e.g. ability, self report or other people's perspectives)
2. How will I use the results?
3. How much does it cost?
4. Who is going to be conducting the measurement and feedback?
5. What will I do after I have the results?

Keep in mind that measurement is only one part of the puzzle. It's important that any measurement device is supported by clear and careful follow-up.

In Summary: My Opinion of the Available Measures

*   The 'whole-life' focus of the Bar-On EQ-i, MEIS and EI-360 gives them wider use.
*   The Bar-On EQ-i currently provides the most comprehensive measurement of someone's emotional intelligence.
*   The MEIS ability model of John Mayer, Peter Salovey and David Caruso shows the most promise for future application, particularly as further data is collected showing the link between the ability scales and effective performance in a job or in relationships.
*   The web-enabled EI-360 of the Institute of Health and Human Potential is easy to use and administer. Whilst it lacks the psychometric depth and research properties of the others, it is useful when used in conjunction with either the ability scales or the self-report Bar-On EQ-i to provide 360-degree feedback information.

So to finish up, a quick quiz on the 'whole life' schools of emotional intelligence:

Quick Quiz No. 3

1. How many different schools of emotional intelligence have I described?

Answer: _____

2. Which 3 measures are focused on someone's 'whole life' not just work?

Answer: _____

3. Who is the author of the EQ-i™?

Answer: _____

4. Who are the authors of the MEIS™?

Answer: _____

5. Who is the author of the EI-360™?

Answer: _____

6. Which of the available measures can be used in recruitment?

Answer: _____

7. Which of the three measures described is fully web-enabled?

Answer: _____

8. Which measure is the only actual 'ability test' of emotional intelligence?

Answer: _____

9. Which measures require trained users?

Answer: _____

10. Which is the instrument that Daniel Goleman is associated with?

Answer: _____

Once you have checked your answers, we'll move onto measuring your emotional intelligence in Chapter 4.

> 'Emotional lessons – even the most deeply implanted habits
> of the heart learned in childhood – can be reshaped.
> Emotional learning is lifelong.'[xv]
> *Daniel Goleman*

Chapter 4

Measuring Your Emotional Intelligence

This chapter provides:

- A brief measurement of your emotional intelligence using questions taken from MEIS, one of the well-known measures of emotional intelligence reviewed in Chapter 3.
- An opportunity for you to prioritise your reading of the rest of this book by completing a review of the main feelings in different areas of your life.

What follows are a few sample questions taken from the Multifactor Emotional Intelligence Scale (MEIS), copyright Drs. John Mayer, Peter Salovey and David Caruso, reproduced here with permission. These items are illustrative of the type of items that appear on this ability test of emotional intelligence. Of course, the actual MEIS contains many such items, and these few sample items are meant only to provide you with a concrete way of understanding how it is possible to measure the abilities of emotional intelligence. This will give you a snapshot of your emotional intelligence and it may spur you to want to complete the full assessment after reading this book.

Activity 1: Quick assessment of your emotional intelligence using MEIS

Instructions: Complete each of the five Tasks below, following the instructions for each task.

TASK 1: *IDENTIFYING EMOTIONS*

Instructions: In this part, you will read a story and indicate the emotions which you believe the person telling the story was *feeling*.

This story comes from the mother of a 27-year-old daughter.

Last night my 27 year-old daughter called to announce that she was getting engaged to her boyfriend of 8 months. She sounded very excited and quite happy. She wanted me to be happy for her, and she asked me what I thought. I met her boyfriend several times and I strongly feel that he is bad news. He treats her poorly and puts her down a lot – even in front of me. I don't think he realises it, which makes it all seem worse. My daughter is a wonderful person, and she deserves much better.

How is the person telling the story feeling? Now circle your answer on each of the five feelings below.

Scoring (1 = Definitely not present, 5 = Definitely present)					
Ashamed	1	2	3	4	5
Accepting	1	2	3	4	5
Fearful	1	2	3	4	5
Depressed	1	2	3	4	5
Loving	1	2	3	4	5

TASK 2: *USING EMOTIONS*

Instructions: For this part, you create a mild emotion, which you then use to solve problems. The goal is NOT to generate strong emotions. You will be asked to imagine an event in the future that could make you feel a certain way. Then, while you are feeling that way, you will rate your feelings. If you have problems doing this, then just answer the questions as you think you would if you could really imagine the feeling.

Now, imagine an event that could make you feel somewhat excited. Imagine this event until you feel mildly excited.

Describe your feelings on *each* of the following four scales, circling your answer.

Dull	1	2	3	4	5	Sharp
Pleasant	1	2	3	4	5	Unpleasant
Good	1	2	3	4	5	Bad
Sweet	1	2	3	4	5	Sour

TASK 3: *UNDERSTANDING EMOTIONS (1)*

Instructions: Some emotions are more complex than others and consist of two or more simple emotions. In this part, you will be asked to indicate which simple emotions form a more complex emotion.

Sadness most closely combines which two emotions? *(Select the best answer by circling it.)*

1. **Anger and surprise**

2. **Fear and anger**

3. **Disappointment and acceptance**

4. **Remorse and joy**

TASK 4: *UNDERSTANDING EMOTIONS (2)*

Instructions: You will read a story about two people. Then, you will be asked to indicate how the two people would feel.

John tells his long-time girlfriend Mary that he loves her. Indicate how likely it would be for John to experience these emotions.

How does John feel?

Circle your best answer on each of the two lines.

Scoring (1 = Extremely likely, 5 = Extremely unlikely)					
Loving toward Mary	1	2	3	4	5
Wondering if the relationship would work	1	2	3	4	5

How does Mary feel?

Circle your best answer on each of the two lines.

Scoring (1 = Extremely likely, 5 = Extremely unlikely)					
Loving toward John	1	2	3	4	5
Curious about why he is expressing love now.	1	2	3	4	5

TASK 5: *MANAGING EMOTIONS*

Instructions: You will read about a situation involving another person and some possible actions. The task is to indicate how effective each action would be to cope with the emotions in the story.

You have been dating the same person for several months and feel very comfortable. Lately, you are thinking that this relationship may be the one, and although living together hasn't been discussed, you are assuming that it is a real possibility. The last thing you expected was the phone call you just received saying that the relationship is over. You have lost the love of your life.

How effective would each of the following be in resolving the real issues? Rate *every* action by circling your answer on each line.

Scoring (1 = Extremely ineffective, 5 = Extremely effective)					
You would do some enjoyable things for yourself. When you feel ready, you'll talk to your friends who have offered to set you up with someone.	1	2	3	4	5
You would call the other person and find out what happened. You would try and figure out what you did, and if it was nothing, why you chose this person to start with and why you didn't see that there were problems with the relationship.	1	2	3	4	5
The best way to cope with this terrible blow is to do whatever you can to block it out and not let it get to you any more than it has. You would throw yourself into your work or some activity and then try to put it behind you.	1	2	3	4	5
You would feel the pain of this loss, and express how you felt to someone who you trusted.	1	2	3	4	5

In total, you should have 18 circled answers.

Expert Advice on Interpreting Your Scores[i]

Of course, you are probably wondering how you did on this 'test'! If you want to measure your emotional intelligence, you will have to take a real test of emotional intelligence such as the MEIS, since these few questions cannot yield a reliable or valid measure of emotional intelligence. I also want to caution the reader not to use these few sample items to gauge the emotional abilities of other people, and especially, not to consider these few items for use in coaching or research programmes.

There are better or worse answers on the MEIS. However, often you receive points for a correct response for different answers. This is due to the fact that people can experience conflicting emotions, but also to the fact that the MEIS takes into account that we can't assign exact numbers to emotions. Thus, rating *anger* a 4 or 5 can result in a similar score. Here is an explanation of the scoring.

TASK 1: *IDENTIFYING EMOTIONS*

The woman does not sound ashamed, so a rating of 1 or 2 may fit this situation the best. She is not accepting of the situation (1 or 2). She is worried about her daughter and what will happen, so fear is present (perhaps a 3, 4 or even 5). She may feel like she is losing her daughter and perhaps powerless to change the situation. Thus, she can feel depressed (a 3 to 5 rating). She seems to care deeply for her "wonderful" daughter and feels loving (3 to 5) towards her.

TASK 2: *USING EMOTIONS*

You were asked to imagine an event that could make you feel somewhat excited.

Many people have a lot of trouble with this type of emotional intelligence test question. They wonder just what is going on here and what they are being asked to do. Other people find it extremely difficult to feel something they don't feel. But, this is the exact point of this type of synaesthesia question: to get into a mood and to reason with it.

What does 'excited' feel like? The easiest way to answer the question is to feel excited. Recalling an exciting event is one way to generate such a feeling. Next, emotions have a certain feel to them. Positive emotions tend to be more pleasant and warmer than negative emotions.

In this example, Excitement is an intense feeling. It is not a low, *dull* feeling, but more of a well-defined emotion, and *sharp*. Excitement is a *pleasant* feeling, one that most people enjoy experiencing. Likewise, it is a *good* feeling and an 'up' feeling. Excitement is *sweet* whereas an emotion such as disgust is bitter.

TASK 3: *UNDERSTANDING EMOTIONS (1)*

Sadness implies that we have experienced a loss. The mourning that follows a loss allows us to begin to cope with the loss and to start the healing process. We are disappointed by a loss. Maybe we had expected a different outcome. But, we also have to accept the loss. We know that it is gone from us and that we cannot retrieve it. So the best answer is 3, d*isappointment & acceptance*.

TASK 4: *UNDERSTANDING EMOTIONS (2)*

How does John feel?

Best answers:

> Loving toward Mary: 5
> Wondering whether the relationship will work out: 2

John clearly loves Mary. Although it is possible that John is actively wondering whether the relationship is going to work and last, we have no information to indicate that this is *likely*. It's a long-term relationship as well. This is a key element of emotional decision-making: we must base our decisions on the available information and try not to engage in thinking of possibilities when we have no further information. This is not to say that imagination is a bad thing! Instead, we find that people often impose their own wishes, desires and emotions into situations and then use these incorrect data sources to solve the emotional problem.

How does Mary feel?

Best answers:

> Loving toward John: 4
> Curious about why he is expressing his love now: 4

Mary is likely to love John. Does she really? Of course, we don't know, but we can say with some assurance that it is likely. They have a long-term relationship going here. Because of this, there is some chance that she is a bit perplexed as to why John is professing his love. It's usually not an everyday event in a longer-term relationship.

TASK 5: *MANAGING EMOTIONS*

What is the best response in this situation? It depends upon your goals. If you want to drown out your feelings, then *ignoring the situation* would be your best alternative. But repressed emotions usually come back later. Going out and *having a good time* can allow you to calm down and cool off. But putting off the hard work of emotional thinking is not likely to result in a positive outcome. *'Taking' the emotion* and realising that emotions are signals and sources of information, we can begin to approach the surface, and address the underlying problems.

I hope that this has given you an insight into your emotional intelligence.

David Caruso

So now that you have completed a measurement of your emotional intelligence, the question is, do you manage emotions or do they manage you? The next activity will help you to identify your priorities in your reading of the rest of the book.

Activity 2: Feelings assessment

In this activity you are asked to review a total of sixty feelings words (see following pages). This activity is designed to provide an opportunity to think carefully about eight areas of your life and to identify where you are feeling positive and where you are feeling most negative.

When we are not used to being tuned into our feelings, we might wrongly assume that we have the same feelings wherever we are and whomever we are with.

You are asked to place a tick in the appropriate column to indicate the places in your life where you experience each particular emotion. So, for instance, ask yourself, 'Do I feel apathetic in my partner relationship?' If the answer is 'yes', place a tick in the fourth box provided. Then ask yourself; do I feel apathetic about my family? If the answer is 'no', leave the square blank.

Reviewing Your Responses

Now, go back over this list and circle the ticks that are helping you – helping you to live the life you want. Sometimes negative feelings can be useful too – they are a guide and a signal to change things. Put the total in box (a). Then count up the rest (ones that are getting in the way) and put the total in box (b).

In the bottom row, write your order of priority for reading the remaining chapters of this book: number the columns 1 to 8, based on your totals in (a) and (b).

'There are two worlds: the world we measure with line and rule,
and the world we feel with our hearts and imaginations.'
James Henry Leigh Hunt (1784–1859)

Feelings	Personal life				Work life			
	Myself	Family	Friends	Partner relationships	Career	Teams	Leadership	Decision-making
1 Apathetic								
2 Cared for	✓	✓	✓	✓				
3 Belittled								
4 Appreciated				✓				
5 Weak							✓	
6 Calm								
7 Bored								
8 Cheerful								
9 Threatened				✓	✓			
10 Confident								
11 Controlled								
12 Considerate								
13 Criticised								
14 Curious								
15 Disappointed								
16 Delighted								
17 Disheartened								
18 Enthusiastic								
19 Distressed								
20 Excited								
21 Empty*		✓						

Feelings	Personal life				Work life			
	Myself	Family	Friends	Partner relationships	Career	Teams	Leadership	Decision-making
22 Glad								
23 Disrespected								
24 Grateful								
25 Forced								
26 Fortunate								
27 Sad								
28 Happy								
29 Distrusted								
30 Healthy								
31 Hopeless								
32 Hopeful								
33 Under-estimated								
34 Joyful								
35 Insecure					✓	✓	✓	
36 Optimistic								
37 Scared								
38 Passionate								
39 Unheard								
40 Peaceful								
41 Lonely								
42 Loved								

Feelings	Personal life				Work life			
	Myself	Family	Friends	Partner relationships	Career	Teams	Leadership	Decision-making
43 Misunderstood								
44 Pleased								
45 Neglected								
46 Proud								
47 Invalidated								
48 Respected								
49 Mocked								
50 Satisfied								
51 Interrogated								
52 Strong								
53 Judged								
54 Understood								
55 Resentful								
56 Tender								
57 Tearful								
58 Valued								
59 Unsupported								
60 Warm-hearted								
(a) TOTAL number of circled ticks.								
(b) TOTAL left uncircled.								
Priority								

Part 2
Personal Life

'Your diamonds are not in far distant mountains or
in yonder seas; they are in your own backyard, if you but dig for them.'
Russell Conwell (1843–1925)

'The people we are in relationship with are always a mirror, reflecting our own
beliefs, and simultaneously we are mirrors, reflecting their beliefs. So relationship is one of the most powerful tools for growth ... if we look honestly at our
relationships we can see so much about how we have created them.'
Shakti Gawain

Introduction to Part Two

The main 'research centre' for increasing our emotional intelligence is in our personal lives – with our family, our friends, our partners, and with ourselves. It is also the place where we are likely to get the biggest payback from increasing our emotional intelligence. The relationships that we have give us immediate 'feedback' on the extent to which we are really able to bond with others and deal with emotions. Often it is in our personal lives that we experience mismanaged emotions and have practice in dealing with other people's emotions and the emotional undertones in relationships! Over the years, it is amazing how many people have said to me that they can somehow keep the 'public face' while at work but that it is their family and close friends who really know them.

John is a career civil servant who has worked in a central government department for years. When we started to talk about emotional intelligence, the first example he gave was how he screams at his teenage daughters – 'I just cannot get through to them except by shouting.' So I asked him which feelings he thought his girls were most experiencing at this point in their lives. He stopped and thought about it and said, 'Well, fear of course, and probably anxiety and uncertainty about their own identity.' So then I asked, 'What is it that you most need when you're experiencing fear, anxiety and uncertainty?' The penny dropped. They were most needing reassurance, comfort and reinforcement of who they really are. This was exactly what he was *not* giving them.

Notice in the last paragraph that the emotions are described as 'feelings'. Before going into each of the chapters in Part Two, I want to say a few words about how to express a feeling. Many of the activities in Parts Two and Three require you to focus on the feelings that you experience.

In a world of over-analysing and rational thought, we have not learned how to express feelings. Feelings are usually a three-word sentence which starts with 'I feel' and ends with a feeling word, for example 'I feel sad.' It's that simple. However, we often hear feelings expressed as thoughts, things or behaviours and this limits our self-expression or possibilities to communicate our feelings. These are two classic ways not to express feelings:

1. I Feel Like … (a Behaviour, a Thing)

I feel like …

When we use the stem 'I feel like' we very often complete the sentence with a behaviour or thing:

- 'I feel like … going out' (*a behaviour*)
- 'I feel like … screaming' (*a behaviour*)
- 'I feel like … saying nothing' (*a behaviour*)
- 'I feel like … a lemon' (*a thing*)
- 'I feel like … a gooseberry' (*a thing*)
- 'I feel like … a drink' (*a thing*)

These are *not* feelings.

2 I Feel That …(a Thought)

I feel that …

The stem 'I feel that' usually ends up expressing a thought, rather than a feeling:

- 'I feel that … you are wrong' (*a thought*)
- 'I feel that … he is going to win' (*a thought*)
- 'I feel that … you have no idea' (*a thought*)
- 'I feel that … you are not listening to me' (*equivalent to blaming someone else for the condition: better to say, 'I feel unheard'*)
- 'I feel that … I am being excluded' (*better to say, 'I feel excluded*)

These are feelings which are communicated as thoughts, thus limiting their impact.

In Appendix 7, there is a list of over 1,500 'feelings' words. One task that psychologists have set their minds to is to identify the most crucial emotions in life and what relationship they have to each other. Paul Ekman (Professor of Psychology, University of California, San Francisco), identified the following six primary emotions: Happiness, Surprise, Disgust, Fear, Anger, Sadness.

There are four chapters in Part Two: the first focuses on our relationship with ourselves, and then come our relationships with family, friends and partners. Each chapter starts with a description of one key emotion that is often absent in the particular area of life; it then describes emotionally intelligent relationships in action and also shows you the contrast with low emotional intelligence. Then there are two key activities for you to work through in this area of life. Enjoy!

Chapter 5
Myself

Serenity

Serenity sounds quiet and constant
It looks perfect and unsoiled
It is sure and unwavering
So where can I find the calm
The space they call serenity?
It isn't in my face a bit worn, but happy
It isn't in mind sometimes sad, sometimes carefree
But there is a very small place inside my body
Quiet, perfect, sure
I look forward to the day
When I feel it in my veins running freely
Renewing me to serenity

By Alex Bird, reproduced with permission

During the personal emotional intelligence programme that I run, I ask participants to create two projects for increasing their emotional intelligence – one in relationships and one in their community. Recently one participant described how she was feeling about herself and she concluded that she had to do some work on herself before she could really be in relationship with other people. This is how she relayed it to me:

> I seem to be a good person. I am able to have a good relationship with my mum and increasingly with my dad. I have been with my partner for twelve years but we don't seem to be going anywhere. I'm not sure what it is that I really want any more – I seem to have just continued to live with the people that happen to be there. My partner and I are more like housemates – we each do our own thing during the week and we come together some weekday evenings and part of the weekend to be around other people. I'm just not sure what I want any more. I'm not depressed or unhappy, I'm just not sure what I want to create in my life. I think I might need to create a crisis in my own life in order to move on.

In many walks of life, having a strong concept of who you are is a real asset.

> I recently met the Managing Director of a London-based film company that had recently secured millions of pounds of venture capital. He had attended seventy-five meetings where he had received a 'no' to his proposal for funding and at the close of his seventy-sixth meeting he was given a 'yes'. This demanded huge amounts of self-confidence and being able to deal with the failures without falling apart. Whilst he said that he found it tough, he never gave up. And this was at a time when he was experiencing the break-up of his marriage and he had recently become a father.

This chapter focuses on our relationship with ourselves and on the emotional content of how we deal with our own life. Many of us don't take time to undertake this sort of reflection.

Activity 3: Your life seen from a helicopter

In Chapter 1 we saw that the analogy of a house can be used to focus on emotional intelligence – how are you around other *people*, to what extent do you understand your *inner workings* and how do you cope with *bad weather*? This activity can help you to understand the *inner workings* of your emotions and the *people* around you.

This activity is designed to give you a process for taking a snapshot of all areas of your life as if you were in a helicopter, looking down at your life, seeing the whole landscape of relationships, activities and scenery.

Take a large sheet of paper and use it to focus on six areas of your life:

- intimate relationships
- family
- leisure
- friendships
- work
- relationship to self.

Draw what these areas of your life are like, using pictures only. From a helicopter it is the *whole area* that you see and what it is like, not the detail of the words or the specific people. For instance, are your friendships a playground of children having fun, or more like a nightclub with loud music? Is your intimate relationship a beautiful, peaceful lake or a thick, dangerous jungle with wild tigers ready to eat you up? Is your work a source of energy or is it a hospital for the sick? Is your family a united football team or warring factions of a tribe? Is your relationship to yourself like a mirror (what you see is what there is) or is what you see someone else's image?

You can be very creative with this activity. It will help you to clarify what your whole life is like right now. Identify where you have the strongest negative feelings, that might signal a need for change.

Activity 3 should have helped you to take stock of how you're feeling about yourself. The next activity is designed to make this more specific.

Activity 4: Charting your moods

Inspired by Chuck Wolfe[i]

Keep a mood journal, listing how you feel at particular times. Start now! Use the chart below, placing a number next to each word to identify how you are feeling right now.

I feel ...

Not at all	1	2	3	4	5	6	7	Very

Appreciated	Bored	Belittled
Cared for	Controlled	Grateful
Cheerful	Misunderstood	Judged
Confident	Neglected	Mocked
Considerate	Disheartened	Hopeless
Curious	Lonely	Busy
Delighted	Punished	Pressured
Enthusiastic	Imprisoned	Disappointed
Excited	Disrespected	Criticised
Fortunate	Uncared for	Threatened
Glad	Understood	Underestimated
Happy	Forced	Encroached upon
Healthy	Strong	Insecure
Hopeful	Tearful	Stressed
Joyful	Distrusted	Distressed

Loved	Invaded	Interrogated
Passionate	Concerned	Hyperactive
Peaceful	Scared	Sad
Pleased	Unimportant	Unheard
Proud	Calm	Invalidated
Satisfied	Respected	Resentful
Tender	Empty	Weak
Valued	Unsupported	Unseen
Warm-hearted	Apathetic	Optimistic

You may wish to repeat this analysis on different days, weeks and months and notice the patterns that emerge – for instance, are there particular activities that create low feelings for you? What are trends in your mood journal?

Think of three situations that help you to feel good.

Try to remember times when you felt really happy. For example:

- you are on holiday, in a favourite spot, with favourite scenery and favourite weather, with your favourite person
- your boss surprises you with an unexpected bonus
- you win the lottery
- you're speaking to a friend on the phone and sharing recent news and laughing together
- you're laughing so hard you can hardly control yourself
- you're watching a sad film with a very happy ending
- someone tells you they love you and you feel warm all over
- you come top of the class in school/college/university
- you tell a hilarious joke and everyone laughs
- you win a prize in a competition.

Now close your eyes, recall these times and hold these happy feelings for as long as you can. Some people find this useful to do with background music. If you think it might help, find some music that is conducive and set aside a few minutes a day to generate positive emotion. This is based on a technique called 'Heart Lock-in' created by HeartMath.

Think of three situations that make you feel bad.

Sometimes bad feelings are not all bad. (Mike Myers, creator of Austin Powers, wrote his first story following the death of his father. His feelings of pain inspired him to write the whole story in a period of two weeks.) But these situations can give us clues on what to avoid, so identify the ones that you want to avoid and the ones that help you.

'The only part of us that is 100% honest is our emotions.'
Anonymous

Chapter 6

My Family

True Love

Love is
really caring
about someone
like I care for you.

Unconditional love is
caring about you
even when
you're really
angry with me.

Love is
being close to you
as your best friend.

Unconditional love is
being far away from you
when that's
what you need.

Love is
wanting the best
and believing the best
for you.

Unconditional love is
not knowing what 'best' is.

Love is being there for you
in your moments of sadness and
pain

Unconditional love is
resisting the temptation to make
you feel better

By Geetu Orme

During my early twenties, when I had just started working in the personal development field, I was often on the lookout for 'problems'. I sought out things I could have an influence on – particularly things like stuck relationships or where someone had recently had a death in their family and I could be part of their support (as I was trained in bereavement counselling). The funniest example of this 'keenness' was in relation to my own family. One day I decided that it was time to sort out my family – there had been one particularly awful family row and I set my mind on having a 'family workshop'. You can imagine the surprise when each member of my family (brother, sister-in-law, mother, father and sister) received a letter inviting them to a family workshop at my house in two weeks' time with the objective of 'becoming a better family'. I now know that they had a laugh at my expense, and that I was trying to fix my family before I contemplated my own role in the problems that were occurring. Well, all I can say is that this is *not* the way to fix your family! It might provide entertainment for your parents and siblings but it is not to be recommended.

Emotional intelligence takes a bigger, a more daily and deeper commitment to dealing with family life as it evolves, and the focus of this commitment will be different in different phases of life. Emotions have a massive role to play, as families create the situations that, for some of us, provide material for practising emotional management and expressing who we really are. This chapter provides some examples of high and low emotional intelligence in families, and two activities – the first to develop awareness, insight and conversation about things that happen in life, and the second to focus on what we can learn about humanity.

I used to spend a lot of time with a family in Worcestershire – a family of three siblings: two brothers and a sister, each with their respective partners and families. They had had much sadness in their lives – their parents had both died early in life. When I used to see them for weekends, I was often struck by how tiring it was to be in their company. Everyone seemed to talk at once and everyone seemed to have something more important to say than the person who was speaking, so as soon as someone else started talking, the three siblings interrupted each other, and this happened constantly, all day. I soon learned that the best way to conserve my energy was to say nothing and to leave them to it.

A friend of mine has relayed to me what her early family life was like, particularly in her early childhood. Her mother was the heart of the family; her father was more withdrawn and remote from both his wife and the four children. Every Christmas he used to open his presents and the first thing he would say is 'Oh dear dear dear'. When it was his wife's birthday and the children had planned a special meal out for her in a restaurant, he stayed at home, didn't take part in the birthday celebrations, and told others later that he didn't join them because 'he wasn't hungry'. Whilst all four children in this family have now accepted their Dad more as he is, you won't be surprised to know that the mother and father separated years ago – the father lives alone and the mother is happy with her life. She still has close relationships with her four children; she is now in her mid sixties, attractive, kind and generous. She has recently lost a lot of weight and looks marvellous. However, thinking about her earlier life, you can't help but think that this family could have been better able to cope with a dose of emotional intelligence.

And yet the power of families is incredible.

A few years ago I met a man called Stewart who I quite liked. We met through a mutual friend who suggested that we go out together. On the evening we met, I had just run in a half marathon and was feeling a little worse for wear but still excited about meeting him. When we had dinner together, I thought we were getting on famously. At the end of the evening, he was very non-committal about meeting again and I was a bit puzzled. Anyway, he phoned me a few days later and said that he had decided that whilst we were getting on really well, he didn't want to see me romantically. At the time, I thought this was 'odd' but didn't think too much of it. Anyway, Stewart and I both stayed single for another year. We spent a lot of time together – took up paragliding, shared sociable times with our respective friends, went to parties, went out for meals. He helped me move into my new house and planned a house-warming barbecue on my first night there. Stewart was a special friend. One year after I had met him, he told me in a drunken state that he was totally stunned when he first met me and was totally shocked that I was Indian. He said that, having spoken to me on the phone, he didn't have a second thought that I was anything other than white. He said that, knowing his parents as he does, they would never accept a non-Caucasian into their family. I was completely gob-smacked! Whilst I had accepted Stewart as a close friend, I had no idea of the 'bigotry' that he had grown up with. What he was effectively saying was that he could accept me as long as I was a friend and nothing else. And whilst he pinned it on his parents, he was also describing his own values.

Stewart is still single, and still searching. I am struck by how powerful the influence of the family is for many people, whether there are strong bonds or no bonds.

Once when I was on a train travelling between London and Manchester, I overheard the most outrageous conversation between a mother and a child. The mother screamed at her five-year-old daughter, 'You are so awful, I wish you had never been born. You're just such a pain. I hate you!' She also swore at her child. This mother was totally unaware of what she was saying and didn't notice that two people stood up and moved to another carriage. Of course, I have no idea what prompted this or what she had experienced in her life, but the behaviour that her child was learning from her mother was direct and public humiliation in front of others, abusive language and inappropriate anger.

Remember that children have just as much need to be heard as do adults (if not more).

So how do we improve emotional intelligence in families?

The following activities involve television and art as a way to focus on understanding emotions. Both of them require high emotional intelligence on your part, to persuade others in your family that it will be worthwhile to do the activities, then to actually do them and then to learn from them. You will need to make a decision based on your readiness to attempt this with your family, knowledge of your family, the age of the children and the maturity of the adults.

Activity 5: Using TV to increase emotional intelligence

Inspired by the work of Hendrie Wiesenger, author of Emotional Intelligence at Work.

This activity takes a day-to-day happening, watching television, and structures an activity that will make it more productive and meaningful. Hendrie Weisinger's own parents used this approach with films and serials like *Bonanza, Lassie* and *Alfred Hitchcock Presents*. He has since used it for his children, aged fifteen and eight,[i] and reports that it has helped to develop their problem-solving and their ability to manage their feelings, to increase their sensitivity for others, deal with adversity, and cope with fears.

First of all, make a commitment to watch a film, or an episode of a serial, that is a favourite of someone in your family. (You could take it in turns, and make sure that you've covered everyone's favourites.) Home movies of the family are not appropriate. Ahead of time, think what particular questions you could ask relating to the emotional content of the film or episode.

When watching:

1. Ask yourself and the others, 'If you had to make up the story, what would happen next?'
2. Share your own feelings about the story and the characters.
3. When main characters in the story are facing difficulties, ask yourself and the others, 'How would you handle that situation?'
4. Throughout, ask yourself and the others, 'What would you do in that situation?'
5. At the end, discuss how the main character could have handled the problem differently. What would have happened?

Throughout, share your feelings.

Activity 6: Seeing modern art

This activity was inspired by conversations that I had with Jo Manby, Assistant Curator at the Lowry – the UK's largest arts project which received millions of pounds in lottery funding. This activity involves buying a book on modern art or visiting a local art gallery. There are a number of well-known artists who have a lot to teach us about emotions and about our humanity.

With your family, visit a modern art gallery or (if you are not close to an art gallery) buy a book on modern art and look up the following artists:

- Paul Klee (1879–1940)
- Joan Miró (1893–1983)
- Marc Chagall (1887–1985)
- Pablo Picasso (1881–1973)
- Wassily Kandinsky (1866–1944)

Review some paintings by these artists and discuss together:

1. What do you each see in each of the pictures?
2. What do you think the artist was communicating in their choice of medium?
3. What does each artist communicate about what it means to be human?

> 'If you cannot get rid of the family skeleton,
> you may as well make it dance.'
> *George Bernard Shaw (1856–1950)*

Chapter 7

My Friendships

JOY

J is for Joy
The girl with the corn-coloured hair
Skipping through a field
in a 1950's hardback
A hand-me-down
from my parents'
Carefree childhood

And I was jealous of Joy
How can I be like her?
I asked myself
How can I have that smile?

Those rosy cheeks
Me, with so many worries
Things on my mind

But now I know that Joy is not a picture
Not an ideal girl
To chase and catch
Joy is within me
If only I release it
Like letting free
Beautifully coloured butterflies
For others to see and enjoy.

By Russell Speirs, reproduced with permission

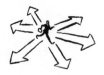

This chapter focuses on friendships – the people you choose to share fun times with, the people you go out with and do things with for companionship. At the end of it, you should have a better understanding of the qualities of excellent friendships, and be able to identify the specific emotions that prevent us from creating great friendships. You will also have identified what specific things you want to do to create more fun in your friendships.

My friend Lea said to me, 'I have lots of friends but the true friends are the ones I can really laugh with.' Friendships need joy – without it a friendship can seem heavy, low and just plain boring. This links very well to the science discussed in Chapter 2. You may want to reflect and ask: Which are your main friendships? Are they 'energy-creating' or 'energy-depleting'? Are they true friendships or are they a carry-over from a past time in your life?

The feeling of joy, for me, is so linked to friendships. Apart from our parents, friendships represent a key 'bonding' relationship that we experience early in life. But we don't always sustain good friendships over a number of years; it's easy to grow away from the friends we had years ago. Some people just exist within their friendships – a friend of mine said to me recently, 'Sometimes I just keep going with my friends because they happen to be living in the same town. We still see each other but I'm not sure if I really want to hang out with them any more.' There are friends, and there are real friends. So what is it that distinguishes emotionally intelligent friendships – what role do *emotions* play in friendships? What is it like when emotional intelligence is missing?

Within the last ten years, I've moved house three times and each time I've employed the services of a small local removal company, owned by Mick. During my first move, I struck up conversation with Mick over a cup of tea when he and his helper Steve were taking a short break. I asked Mick how his wife and child were and how his business was going. At this point in the conversation, both Steve and Mick went silent and blushed. I wondered what I had said. In a slow, shaky voice, Mick explained that his wife had left him, and was now living with Steve, his 'best mate'. I turned to look at the Steve who was there, hoping that Mick was referring to someone else. But it was this Steve who Mick was referring to. Here were these two adult men, with this 'uncomfortable-ness' around them that they were not dealing with. Mick said that he needed Steve as a helper and, regardless of what he had done, he was still a friend of his.

Wow! That is either good emotional management or a mad person out of touch with reality. You decide … However you look at it, these two had continued their working relationship and friendship, yet there was clearly some hurt and anger underneath. I wondered how 'true' their friendship could be if one guy ended up sleeping with his best friend's wife.

My six-year-old niece learned the expression 'I'm not your friend' when she was three years old. It was her way of having a tantrum and letting it be known who she felt was 'on side' and who was not. Her statement was loaded with so much anger and resentment. It was a statement reserved only for people who had been 'mean', who didn't pander to her every want.

From a young age, children are validated or invalidated through their friendships. It is always entertaining to watch two children play together and create their early friendships. A version of this 'I'm not your friend' is when a friend of yours uses blackmail to make you feel bad: 'You would do it if you loved me.'

I grew up in Liberia and have a number of Indian friends from my early years. Many of them come to England en route to different parts of the world and they often telephone my mother and let her know that they are in the UK. They ask for a message to be passed to me, even when my mother suggests that they take the time to telephone me. My view is that if someone wants to speak to me enough, they can telephone me directly. When I don't call, they get upset and start to complain to others. Friends who are not true friends tend to put pressure on each other.

My best friend Alison is someone I have known from school days – sometimes we see each other very regularly and sometimes it can be months before we meet again. What is amazing is how 'uncluttered' our relationship is – we can go months without seeing each other and then just come together and have great conversations and pick up where we left off. We speak on the phone regularly. I know that I can phone her and say anything I like. I know she is there in times of need. I also know that when we are together, we can laugh, cry, enjoy whatever we are doing together (even errands) and sometimes, be quiet in each other's company. Two years ago I ran in the London marathon for Scope, a charity that supports people with cerebral palsy. Alison had agreed to be at the start line with me but on the morning of the race, she looked like 'death warmed up' – pale and ill, having been sick in the night with food poisoning. But she knew how important the day was for me and she was able to put to one side her own terrible feelings and travel twenty-six miles to be at the start line with me. She stayed out in the rain all day, travelling around London on foot and by tube to cheer me on at key spots en route. True friends have a sense of commitment that is noticeable.

I believe that there are two key aspects to focus on in creating emotionally intelligent friendships: these are (1) communication (in terms of having a deep connection) and (2) fun. Activity 7 enables you to analyse the level of *communication* that you have with your friends. Then Activity 8 provides you with a structure for remembering and recreating *fun* times.

Activity 7: TRUST your friend

For many years, I have pondered the word 'trust'. Many people say, 'I just don't trust that person', but what is it exactly that makes up trust? We can love and enjoy friends but we may not be able to trust them with everything – to keep a secret, to return a loan/book/CD, to give up time for us when we need it. Perhaps absolute and enduring trust is a rare thing and we can be tolerant of small breaches of trust such as a friend not turning up at the agreed time (but not every time!). It is my view that good friendships are based on TRUST, where:

T stands for Truthfulness
R stands for Respect
U stands for Understanding
S stands for Support
T stands for Time

Whilst each of us may experience these qualities in different ways, when any of these are missing, the friendship may not last. This activity helps you to check the state of five current friendships. This will help to identify what needs to change in each friendship.

STEP 1: *Take time to review your five most significant friendships against this acronym to see what is missing:*

T	**Truthfulness**	• Expressing emotions – how I feel – as well as facts. • Being honest even about the difficult areas of my life. • Doing what I say. • Avoiding excuses – telling the truth even when it hurts. • Not being afraid of saying it how it is.

Friend 1	Friend 2	Friend 3	Friend 4	Friend 5
Yes/No	Yes/No	Yes/No	Yes/No	Yes/No

R	**Respect**	• Accepting the person, as they are – not wanting to change them. • Listening when the other person speaks. • Asking for their opinion. • Maintaining confidential information. • Checking understanding – not making assumptions. • Accepting what the other person is. • Letting them be themselves, without wanting to control or fix them. • Not blaming them. • Being open and non-judgmental. • Not taking advantage of them – valuing them always. • Asking how they would feel before making decisions that affect them.

Friend 1	Friend 2	Friend 3	Friend 4	Friend 5
Yes/No	Yes/No	Yes/No	Yes/No	Yes/No

U	**Understanding**	• Accepting their flaws. • Being in tune with what they are saying. • Listening intuitively for the 'essence' of what is being said. • Being able to sense when something is wrong before the person even says anything. • Providing constructive feedback. • Asking relevant questions. • Tolerating different views. • Respecting different points of views – yours and others. • Actively listening. • Being able to reiterate what someone is saying, accurately. • Being able to have a real conversation, even when there is no crisis happening.

Friend 1	Friend 2	Friend 3	Friend 4	Friend 5
Yes/No	Yes/No	Yes/No	Yes/No	Yes/No

| S | Support | • Being at the end of a phone, when you're not there in person.
• Making relevant offers of skills and resources.
• Building up each person's confidence.
• Accepting the person, warts and all.
• Asking for help when you need it. Giving help when it is needed.
• Being an advocate for that person.
• Allowing the person to share their problems without judgement.
• Being there in time of need.
• Understanding and contributing to each other. |

Friend 1	Friend 2	Friend 3	Friend 4	Friend 5
Yes/No	Yes/No	Yes/No	Yes/No	Yes/No

| T | Time | • Making time.
• Spending quality time.
• Being able to be silent – and give time to the other person.
• Listening.
• Valuing each other's time.
• Giving space and time. |

Friend 1	Friend 2	Friend 3	Friend 4	Friend 5
Yes/No	Yes/No	Yes/No	Yes/No	Yes/No

STEP 2: *The next time you meet your friends mentioned here, you might want to tell them what you discovered:*

1. The qualities that are present in the friendship.
2. The ones that are missing.

So now you are at the point where you have discovered what is missing; let's now focus on the emotions that might get in the way of achieving TRUST. As you go through these, identify the ones that are stopping you achieve full TRUST in your friendships. Place a tick next to the ones that you experience:

Emotions that can get in the way of Truthfulness:

• *fear* – we may have been hurt before
• *anxiety* – will they like us if they know the whole truth about us?

- *uncertainty* – will they want to know me if they really understood what was going on? Will they find out that I am a sham?

Emotions that can get in the way of Respect:

- *fear* – will they be able to respect me?
- *anger* – I am annoyed at what they have done to me and I just can't forgive them.

Emotions that can get in the way of Understanding:

- *selfishness* – believing that it is more important for others to understand me, believing that I am more important and I have more interesting things to say which stop me listening
- *fear* – will anyone understand me? People are too complex to even try to understand
- *anger* – everyone has been so awful to me, why should I bother?
- *sadness* – if only I had had more love and understanding earlier in my life.

Emotions that can get in the way of Support:

- *fear* – what would it be like if I really loved someone and felt cared for?
- *anger* – everyone has been so awful to me, why should I bother with anyone else? I have been so hard done by.

Emotions that can get in the way of Time:

- *lack of commitment* – do I really believe in this friendship enough to make and keep promises?

Activity 8: Fun fantasies

This activity is designed for you to make a list of all the things you love to do with your friends. These could be regular activities or they could be 'one-offs'. This is a way to create more fun in your friendships – as fun is a useful thing to create.

First write down the ten things you most like to do – then identify with whom, and the date when you last did this activity. This should give you a clear 'To Do' list for your main friendships.

Activity	With whom	Last date I did this
1.		
2.		
3.		
4.		
5.		
6.		
7.		
8.		
9.		
10.		

> 'The only relationships in this world that have
> ever been worthwhile and enduring have been those in
> which one person could trust another.'
> *Samuel Smiles, social reformer (1812–1904)*

Chapter 8

My Partner Relationships

The Love Wish

My love is like a distant call
Resounding in the night;
A far off train; the sound of rain;
a shadow in the light.

My love is like a favourite toy
you leave beside your bed;
A well read book; a passing look;
a thought inside your head.

My love is all around you
- quiet, soft and still;
I only wish I had the gift
to show you how I feel.

By Paul Deemer, reproduced with permission

This chapter is about partner relationships – the intimate relationship that either we are in already or we want to have. You might want to use this chapter to reflect on an existing relationship or to review a relationship that didn't work out. In this chapter you'll find descriptions of emotional intelligence in partner relationships, including examples of where emotional intelligence was lacking. The emotion of anger is one that can often get in the way of relationships, so the first of the two activities included here is focused on taking a 'preventative' approach to situations that might create anger. The second activity helps you to initiate a conversation with the person you love to set the 'tone' for the relationship you really want.

At a recent conference, David Ryback, an adviser on emotional intelligence in the business world, described relationships as going through five stages of love:[i]

1. *romance* – strong physical attraction, a bubble of illusion of togetherness
2. *battle of the sexes* – unmet emotional needs expressed inappropriately or not expressed
3. *negotiation* – of roles, respecting each other's opinions, sharing decision-making, focusing on present and future, time outs, accepting more personal responsibility for your needs together with ongoing communication
4. *mutual acceptance* – from control issues to acceptance
5. *togetherness* – when you really come together and enjoy each other.

So, if you are in a partner relationship with someone, where are you in these five stages?

In a study on successful marriages conducted by Multi-Health Systems in collaboration with the US Air Force in 1996, 1,119 married salespersons were asked to complete the Bar-On Emotional Quotient Inventory (EQ-i) (see Chapter 3) and to rate how satisfied they were with their marriage on a scale of 1 to 5. In addition to having a significantly higher total EQ score, those who indicated that they were more satisfied with their marriage (868) revealed significantly higher scores on the following features, compared with the 251 who reported that they were dissatisfied:[ii]

- *happiness* – the ability to feel satisfied with one's life, to enjoy oneself and others, and to have fun and express positive emotions
- *self regard* – the ability to be aware of, understand, accept, and respect oneself
- *emotional self-awareness* – the ability to recognise and understand one's emotions
- *self-actualisation* – the ability to realise one's potential and to do what one wants to do, enjoys doing and can do
- *social responsibility* – the ability to demonstrate oneself as a cooperative, contributing and constructive member of one's social group
- *reality testing* – the ability to assess the correspondence between what is emotionally experienced and what objectively exists
- *optimism* – the ability to look at the brighter side of life and to maintain a positive attitude, even in the face of adversity.[iii]

Rich Handley, Chief of Air Force Recruits Service, US Air Force, conducted some recent work on men who had been accused of abusing their wives. The Bar-On EQ-i was administered when they were first suspected and then, when cases were substantiated, the EQ scores were compared to average scores for husbands. There were significant differences noted on these seven scales in which the wife abusers all scored low:[iv]

- *emotional self-awareness* – the ability to recognise and understand one's feelings and emotions, differentiate between them, know what caused them and why.
- *independence* – the ability to be self-directed and self-controlled in one's thinking and actions and to be free of emotional dependency
- *problem-solving* – the ability to identify and define personal and social problems as well as to generate and implement potentially effective solutions
- *reality testing* – the ability to assess the correspondence between what is experienced (the subjective) and what really exists (the objective)
- *flexibility* – the ability to adjust one's feelings, thoughts and behaviour to changing situations and conditions
- *stress tolerance* – the ability to withstand adverse events, stressful situations, and strong emotions without 'falling apart', by actively and positively coping with stress
- *optimism* – the ability to look at the brighter side of life and to maintain a positive attitude even in the face of adversity.

So, as you might expect, the data confirm that emotional intelligence matters in relationships. Let's see what happens, first, when it is absent.

My friend Sonia tells a sad story of how her marriage fell apart. For years, she had a sales job that took her all over the country. Her husband would help her with the washing, ironing and getting ready to leave each Sunday. He would help her pack to leave and wave goodbye at the gate when she pulled away – virtually every Sunday for six years. On most Sundays, she would tell him how much she appreciated his help and how much he was an important 'backbone' to her success. For six years, he said nothing about how he was really feeling inside. Then one New Year's Eve, he completely turned on her and – out of the blue – had an angry fit, an emotional explosion that led to him storming out, sobbing uncontrollably and saying how much he hated her being away and how he couldn't cope with it any more. Sadly, they never recovered from this. Sonia was terrified at the strength of his emotion – he was almost violent and out of control. She ended up having to move out. She often wonders how it would have been had he been able to say how he felt – they might have been able to work things out. She still bumps into him from time to time and even now, four years later (he has now remarried and is expecting his first child), he still tells her how much he loves her and cares about her.

The caring actions of Sonia's husband were driven by love but he also had needs that were not being met. Over six years he had stored up feelings of anger and resentment which ultimately he was not able to talk about. This cost them their marriage.

Another friend of mine, Jane, tells the following story of low emotional intelligence.

Last year [she recounts] I met someone called John, a thirty-three-year-old recruitment consultant who I started to date. He was an attractive, lively, intelligent person of exactly the same age as me. In the early days of our relationship I thought we could become close and intimate. One week after I had met him, he joined me for dinner with a couple of my friends. When I was with these friends, we often took it in turns to pay. At the end of the evening he was clearly not a 'happy bunny'. After we had dropped my friends home, he said in an angry tone, 'how *could* you let someone pay for dinner for you – do you have no pride?' He was red in the face, agitated and went 'off' on a whole thing about how important it was to 'pay your share'. He was totally not managing his emotions and totally tuned out of the whole reality of the situation. This was an early signal that he might not be the right person for me – however, I chose to ignore it. Two weeks later, he was annoyed over something trivial again. It was impossible to be in a relationship with him. He was so 'unpredictable'. He taught me a lot about the power of buried emotions – I often wonder what memories were triggered for him, when he and I were together! In the moment when he responded, I was terrified. I froze and was scared to say too much, in case I became the focus of his anger. He caused fear and immobilisation in me. It is often frightening to witness someone else's emotional hijack. When it's you causing the emotional hijack, it can feel so powerful in that moment of rage – it's easy to rationalise to yourself why you are acting this way and later on, way after the moment has passed, this feeling of all-power is often replaced by one of terrible regret and guilt.

So, what are the qualities of relationships that do work out? Whilst I have known a few good role models of excellent partner relationships, there is one couple that really stands out.

Three years ago, I met John and Rachel, a couple now in their sixties who have recently retired from their teaching jobs. I have seen this couple through good times and bad. I spent a Christmas with them, so I've seen them around their family and their friends. I've met them for lunch and spent time with them. The most noticeable thing for me is that they give each other space to talk and their contribution to conversation is balanced (by contrast, I have met many other couples where one person's mouth seems to have been surgically removed and the other person has the verbal strength of at least ten people). Sometimes John leads the conversation and Rachel listens; sometimes Rachel leads and John listens. They have no 'ego' or control of each other. They deal with issues as they happen; they never go to sleep on an argument. This is a couple with high emotional intelligence – dealing with the full range of emotions and dealing with their day-to-day issues as they come up. When I quizzed them about what they do to sustain their relationship, they both agreed that they had decided a number of basic things years before and stuck to them (like never going to sleep on an argument). They said they had talked about everything that had happened in their lives so that they were able to change and evolve together, without one person leaving the other behind – which can happen if two people lead very separate lives.

In the relationships I've described here, you'll have noticed that anger is a theme in the not-so-successful relationships and clarity is a theme in the successful one. The next two activities focus on these themes.

Activity 9: Mismanaged anger

Mismanaged anger, or unexpressed anger, can not only get in the way of relationships but also damage them forever. This activity encourages you to identify your 'hot buttons' – things that your partner does that 'get your goat', that make you lose your temper. In this activity it is recommended that you identify the frequency of these 'hot buttons' and the action you choose to take to move forward. There are three steps involved. I encourage you to complete them now.

STEP 1: List the *situations* that annoy you, frustrate you or anger you about your life with your partner.

STEP 2: Now rank these by adding a number next to each one to identify the *frequency* with which these occur – ranging from 1 (most frequent) to 10 (least frequent).

STEP 3: Now identify what you need to do about each one:
- *forgive* your partner
- *forget* about it
- *discuss* it and express your view
- *acknowledge* that you need to change this; otherwise the relationship will have a cost to it.

Situations	Rank	Action

If you need inspiration to kick-start the process, here are some examples.

Situations	Rank	Action
Being told what to do (I'm not stupid, you know!)	7	Discuss
Being nagged – particularly being told the same thing twice within five minutes	4	Discuss
You not doing what you say you're going to do	8	Forgive
Being late for things that we've been invited to	5	Discuss
Always doing things that you want to	3	Discuss
You being drunk and relying on me to do the driving	6	Forgive/discuss
Not having any free time together	1	Acknowledge
Your mother not wanting to speak to me on the phone	9	Forget
You working late every night of the week	2	Acknowledge
Not enough holidays abroad	10	Discuss

Now that you've identified the 'hot buttons' in your relationship, the ones that you need to 'discuss' or 'acknowledge' require a conversation that provides equal time and space to air your view and your partner's view so that you can try and reach a middle ground. From my experience, many problems can be resolved just by identifying the areas of difficulty.

The next activity provides a more structured approach for having this type of conversation.

Activity 10: Step up

Adapted from material written by Steve Hein – used here with permission.

This activity is designed to help you formulate a conversation with your partner. It covers seven steps to a happier relationship. You may want to work on each step and then discuss it, leave it to one side and then return to it after a few days. Each step involves you and your partner each giving your view. It is not usually a good idea to try to do all these steps in one go. (Rome wasn't built in a day ...)

1. RESPECT, SUPPORT, LISTENING, FRIENDSHIP

What do the words *respect*, *support*, *listening* and *friendship* mean to each of you? What is your evidence that they exist in your relationship?

	My meaning and evidence	My partner's meaning and evidence
Respect		
Support		
Listening		
Friendship		

Here's an example:

	My meaning and evidence	My partner's meaning and evidence
Respect	*letting me speak – silence in the conversation*	*supporting your ambitions – saying that I respect you*
Support	*being a shoulder to cry on – asking if I'm okay*	*letting me do what I want to do with my friends – saying it's okay for me to go to football matches*
Listening	*being able to listen openly – not interrupting*	*picking the moments to talk and the moments to listen – not interrupting*
Friendship	*talking about anything and everything – doing enjoyable things together, sharing interests*	*respecting my friendships – accepting my friends into the house at any time of day or night*

Wherever you notice big differences, discuss what you are both willing to compromise and what you are attached to keeping.

2. LOVE

Discuss how you each believe *love* is shown.

	My love for my partner is shown by:	My partner's love for me is shown by:
In my view		
In my partner's view		

Here's an example:

	My love for my partner is shown by:	My partner's love for me is shown by:
In my view	*listening, giving support, being non judgmental*	*spending time together doing enjoyable things*
In my partner's view	*agreeing to participating in sporting activities as spectator and player*	*living in the same house, doing housework, sharing bills*

Again, pick out the areas that indicate the most difference and discuss them. Many couples don't have this kind of conversation and it can help to avoid problems later on.

3. FEELINGS

On a scale of 0 to 10 where 0 means 'not at all' and 10 means 'very', to what extent do you each feel the following feelings in your relationship? Write a score between 0 and 10 in answer to each feeling. Do your list first and then ask your partner to do theirs.

	Me	My partner
Appreciated*		
Free*		
Respected*		
Understood*		
Valued*		
Judged		
Controlled		

For numbers *below* 7 on the feelings marked with an asterisk, discuss what would help you to feel more appreciated, free, respected, understood and valued. For numbers *above* 3 on the other feelings, discuss what would help you to feel less judged and controlled.

4. CONFLICT

Decide on a method for resolving conflicts (e.g. how quickly you might apologise for something that you've done that you feel bad about; changing demands to preferences; asking yourself what you can do to feel better in a situation; taking responsibility for feelings and not blaming the other person).

My ideal way of resolving conflict: *My partner's way of resolving conflict:*

5. UNHELPFUL PATTERNS

Discuss the unhelpful ways in which you react when you don't get your way (e.g. storm off, withhold affection or support, walk away, say mean things).

My unhelpful patterns: *His/her unhelpful patterns:*

What needs to change to ensure that conflict doesn't lead to violence or unhelpful situations?

6. VALUES
What is important to each of us in terms of values – how we go about our life?

Examples:

Acceptance	Equality	Knowledge	Reality
Admiration	Expression	Logic	Reason
Approval	Faith	Love	Relationships
Attention	Fame	Manners	Religion
Authority	Family	Material wealth	Respect
Cleanliness	Freedom	Obedience	Security
Communication	Friendship	Organisation	Self-sacrifice
Competition	Happiness	Others' opinions	Self-reliance
Conformity	Hard work	Pain avoidance	Serenity
Co-operation	Health	Peace	Status
Distraction	Honesty	Popularity	Success
Education	Image	Power	Tradition
Efficiency	Independence	Punishment	Truth
Entertainment	Integrity	Quiet	Winning

My values: *His/her values:*   *Key differences:*

7. EXPECTATIONS

What do you expect from each other? This might include your expectations in terms of time, friendship, family relationships, quality of listening, etc.

Try not to mix expectations with needs. Needs are based on insecurity and dependency. If you believe you need someone, you probably believe you can't live without him or her. When you love someone, you can be happy even when you are not with that person.

What I expect from my partner: *What my partner expects from me:*

'The emotional health of a couple depends on
how well they air their grievances.'
Daniel Goleman

Part 3

Work Life

'Work is love made visible.'
Kahlil Gibran, The Prophet

Introduction to Part Three

In a North American study by Multi-Health Systems[i] which used the Bar-On Emotional Quotient Inventory to study 4,888 people at work in thirty different types of occupation, overall success at work was put down to five emotional competences:

- *self-actualisation* – the ability to realise one's potential and to do what one wants to do, enjoys doing, and can do

- *happiness* – the ability to feel satisfied with one's life, to enjoy oneself and others, and to have fun and express positive emotions
- *optimism* – the ability to look at the brighter side of life and to maintain a positive attitude, even in the face of adversity
- *self regard* – the ability to be aware of, understand, accept, and respect oneself
- *assertiveness* – the ability to express feelings, beliefs, and thoughts and to defend one's rights in a non-destructive manner.[ii]

In his book *CareerSmarts: Jobs with a Future*, which looked at the best career opportunities, Martin Yate closely examined a number of professions and ranked them on a scale according to whether they require most or least emotional intelligence. He found that some jobs do not require much emotional intelligence, particularly jobs that mainly involve tasks which can be completed by a solitary individual, or by those working with others in fixed or structured ways. He included occupations such as: botanist, biochemist, chef, actuary and forester in the list of jobs requiring less emotional intelligence. At the other end of the spectrum are jobs such as: psychiatrist, social worker, doctor, teacher, human resource manager and nurse – jobs which involve much contact with other people, and that require an ability to empathise with and understand others.

Rick Hughes, an MPhil student at Strathclyde University in Glasgow, has been studying how people manage their emotions at work and which emotions evolve in workplace situations. His findings are interesting. One aspect of his work involved asking people to consider twenty-eight hypothetical workplace scenarios and reflect on a recent event, similar to the hypothetical scenario, and recall the range and intensity of emotions experienced. He found that the following emotions were the most frequently experienced:

- frustration
- anxiety

- fear
- irritation
- depression.[iii]

Whilst he suggests that there may be a greater preoccupation with 'negative' than 'positive' emotions and that there are many internal and external factors that combine to create a negative emotion, he is of the view that there is a 'people dimension' at play here – in other words, that when people work together, it causes them to have certain emotions.

He also found that for sixty per cent of the sample of people studied, the following six work situations had evoked strong emotions:

- the *tension* between managing work and home life
- work *overload* – an unrealistic balance between work tasks and time to complete them
- *company support* – from 'well supported' to 'left out in the cold'
- *promotion* – from 'very positive emotions' to apathetic, e.g. 'about time too'
- *underskilled* – feeling overwhelmed with new skill demands (often people skills)
- *delegation* – sharing work tasks with others who often have different needs, agendas, priorities and pace of work.[iv]

Personally, I have found that our ability to cope with stress and handle pressure is increasingly important, and have experienced this most strikingly in my own career, as I'll explain.

After leaving university I joined the 'fast track' graduate programme of a well-known bank. I was one of twenty-five supposed 'high flyers'. Three months into this programme I was very dissatisfied. I didn't seem to be doing any 'real work' – in the guise of learning, I was observing people but I was not really 'getting stuck in'. I left and took a temporary administration job. The managing director noticed that I was both able and hard-working. After three weeks, he asked me to join the company on a permanent basis.

115

Over the next three years, I worked my socks off – I spent most evenings and some weekends working, and spent a lot of time away, working at different client sites. I was very successful financially – my salary had doubled in the space of two years. I moved to Manchester with the company to help set up a new branch. Three years later, I left this company and set up my own small training consultancy firm. I continued to work hard but this time there was a difference. I took on projects all around the world – I travelled everywhere, and stayed in hotels more than I was ever at home. I took on work that was sometimes paid on half the income that I usually charged. At the time, it seemed like I was doing the right thing. Even when family and friends highlighted that I was doing too much, I was not really interested in their advice. In April 1999, two weeks after a nice holiday in Barbados, I was feeling rested. But the following weekend, when a friend was staying with me, I spiralled out of control and had a hyperactive episode, and ended up in hospital being sedated. My family and friends were shocked and worried sick. I was then misdiagnosed with epilepsy by a laboratory technician who wrote this 'verdict' on an EEG scan that I had had. My family and friends were informed that had I been on my own that night, I could easily have ended up in a police cell. When I sought a second opinion on the diagnosis, a second neurologist re-tested me and found no abnormalities. He analysed the themes of my life and simply put it down to 'doing too much'. I now look back and realise that I was so 'in the fog' that I had no awareness of what I was doing in my life and what my limits were. I'm confident that there are many people in work right now who are heading for their own minor or major breakdowns without any awareness that this could be happening. I don't wish this 'fog' on anyone. But it has really taught me the importance of being in balance and looking after yourself – I don't always apply it to myself, but I'm aware of what is happening so much more than I ever was.

In whatever work you do, whether you're self-employed or on a salary, whether it's a trade, a profession, a customer-facing role, whether you sit at a desk, work outdoors, travel all day or work on a production line, you need emotional intelligence to be happy and fulfilled at work.

Emotional intelligence at work is reflected in how much people like working with you. It's also reflected in how quickly you can get things done and how much you enjoy your work. Where it is missing, work is quite literally 'hard work' for you and for the people you work with. People with lower emotional intelligence end up being hard on themselves and on others, work is completed more slowly and everyone feels resentful.

In this third part of the book, there are four chapters, focused on career, working in a team, leadership and decision-making. Each chapter describes emotional intelligence in action at work and also shows you the contrast with low emotional intelligence. The main focus in this part is on identifying barriers to being effective at work, and on helping you tackle these. At the end of each chapter there are two key activities for you to work through, aimed at helping you deal with the emotional content of what happens at work.

Chapter 9

My Career

Courage

Give me the courage Dad
To show those I care about
that I love them
and not be embarrassed

Give me the courage Dad
To be myself
to say what I think
and not follow the rest

Give me the courage Dad
To accept that I'm wrong
although it might
dent my pride

Give me the courage Dad
To think of others
their needs and emotions
and to look into their eyes

Give me the courage Dad
To be strong in times of trouble
for both myself
and those I love

Give me the courage Dad
To strive for my dreams
without being selfish

Give me the courage Dad
To be like you

The grass is as green as you want it son
And although the forest looks deep
Have belief and courage son
So that you can make that leap

By David Mowat,
reproduced with permission

Courage is a useful quality to have in any career. Changes that are happening in the world of technology require the courage to learn new skills and to attempt new fields. When you are stuck in a particular type of work, courage helps to refocus yourself, perhaps in a new area.

Throughout my career, I have met people who seem to take control of their lives – if things don't work out they take their talent elsewhere. However, I have also met people who don't seem to be able to manage their emotions to help them succeed. If you are in a field that involves starting new things, then your ability to manage emotions will determine your day-to-day success – particularly how you deal with negative emotions when things don't work out or you don't get the promotion that you were hoping for or the contract that you pitched for.

A few months ago, we had a new computer network installed in our company. When the IT sales people first came to find out what we wanted, they were lovely and chatty – they seemed really nice people. They suggested a system for us that would help us to achieve the 'functionality' (as they called it) that we needed. We had a number of different quotes from different IT companies and we decided to go with this particular company as they were local. We had purchased computers from them before and they seemed to know what they were doing. Anyway, we negotiated on price and the system was installed a few weeks later. Two months into using our new system, after we had experienced technical problem after technical problem, the company came back to help us identify what was happening. When the technical people had looked around the new system, they said that one of the reasons we were experiencing difficulties was that the system we had was not in fact the right one for us – we needed a higher-specification system. I had originally suggested this higher-specification system but they had dissuaded us – the salesperson had told us it wasn't necessary, and it was more expensive. We ended up buying the new system, but continued to have a number of difficulties. The company charged us a flat rate per hour every time an engineer was called out to deal with faults, and this has turned out to be a 'limitless pot'. It punished us, the users, for not being competent.

Whilst part of the problem here clearly concerns technical expertise, the important point is that the IT people weren't able to read what was happening. They were too proud to say, 'Sorry, we made a mistake,' and they had no empathy for us as customers and for the frustration we were experiencing. I'm sure you can guess that, after this string of disasters, we found a different local IT provider.

By contrast, Chris is another IT specialist who came to help sort out some of our immediate problems. He was fully aware of all the frustration we had been experiencing and was very clear about what he could do in a day. He helped to get us to the point where we were able to use our computers easily. There was one task he had intended to do for us during a particular day. When he didn't achieve it he amended his bill accordingly to make sure that we would work with him in the future. He was able to read the situation and take appropriate action.

Research on reasons for losing customers has shown that seventy per cent of cases are for reasons related to emotional intelligence, and thirty per cent for other reasons.[i] My view is that you could say the same for careers – seventy per cent of career disasters are for reasons related to emotional intelligence and thirty per cent for other reasons.

Within this chapter, my definition of career success is 'to be all that you can be' and 'success' is not necessarily material. It is about everything being in balance in your life. If you are career-oriented, success might mean achieving your ambitions both materially and professionally, but it is also about satisfying different areas of your life. If you're working in a non-profit organisation, then success might mean making a difference to your community. The two activities which follow enable you to identify the key emotions that you experience at work and to take appropriate action.

Activity 11: Is your career safe?

This activity was inspired by the work of David Caruso and Sigal Barsade (of Yale School of Management) on identifying the main emotions people experience at work and what they are based on.

ASAFE is a useful acronym for focusing on your career. This activity will help you to review the feelings that you experience at work now. You may be employed or self-employed. You may be working in a largely technical role, or managerial. You may be part-time. This review will help you get more in touch with the feelings that you are experiencing right now – the emotions covered are acceptance, sadness, anger, fear and enjoyment.

Review each of these feelings categories and identify the feelings that you have in your current career.

1. ACCEPTANCE – a theme of bonding

How often do you experience the following?

	Never	Sometimes	Often	Very often	Always
Camaraderie with team members or other colleagues	0	1	2	3	4
A positive relationship with a particular person	0	1	2	3	4
Receiving recognition or a promotion	0	1	2	3	4
Praise for a job well done	0	1	2	3	4
People noticing the detail of what you do well	0	1	2	3	4

2. SADNESS – a theme of helplessness

How often do you experience the following?

	Never	Sometimes	Often	Very often	Always
Actions being beyond your control that arouse strong emotions	4	3	2	1	0
Work or project undertakings that are later changed by management	4	3	2	1	0
Failure of another person or project affecting me	4	3	2	1	0
Restructuring or redundancies	4	3	2	1	0
Dull work environment	4	3	2	1	0

3. ANGER – a theme of injustice

How often do you experience the following?

	Never	Sometimes	Often	Very often	Always
Others criticising you	4	3	2	1	0
Your suggestions or comments being ignored	4	3	2	1	0
The organisation/employer acting in an unfair way	4	3	2	1	0
Others not being productive	4	3	2	1	0
Tight deadlines/heavy workload	4	3	2	1	0
Dealing with angry members of the public/angry customers	4	3	2	1	0
Lack of co-operation from others	4	3	2	1	0
Stupidity/ignorance of others	4	3	2	1	0
Not being treated respectfully	4	3	2	1	0

4. FEAR – a theme of uncertainty, especially about one's actions

How often do you experience the following?

	Never	Sometimes	Often	Very often	Always
Your own failure to carry out tasks	4	3	2	1	0
Threats to job continuity in the present position	4	3	2	1	0
Threats to survival at an organisational level	4	3	2	1	0
Threats from your supervisors	4	3	2	1	0
Threats from your customers	4	3	2	1	0
Not expressing your fears to your supervisor/manager	4	3	2	1	0
Threat of an industry downturn	4	3	2	1	0

5. ENJOYMENT – a theme of success

How often do you experience the following?

	Never	Sometimes	Often	Very often	Always
Enjoyment from the work itself	0	1	2	3	4
Positive actions from your superiors	0	1	2	3	4
Positive actions from your peers or subordinates	0	1	2	3	4
Fun at work	0	1	2	3	4
Laughter	0	1	2	3	4

Conclusion

Add up your scores. If you have a score that is between 62 and 124, consider yourself lucky. If you have a score of between 31 and 61, you may want to initiate conversations with your supervisor/manager to see what can be done to make your career happier. If your score is below 31, you may want to ask yourself serious questions about whether this is the right job for you.

Activity 12: Taking action

From the analysis you've carried out in Activity 11, you will be aware that some of the emotions you experience are created by you and some of them are the effects of other people's actions. However, your response to what happens is directly in your control. Looking at this very simply, there are only three possible actions to take. The first two involve only yourself and the third involves what you do in relation to other people. Review each of the following questions and identify what you most need to do right now in your career.

SELF: Do I need to do more
work on identifying what
I really want from my job
and my career?   _____

SELF: Do I need to manage
my own emotions to make
the best of what I have?   _____

OTHERS: Do I need to initiate
a conversation with someone
else (my boss, a colleague,
a friend) to discuss: _____

What is not working?   _____

                                        _____

                                        _____

                                        _____

What would I like to change,
with their help?   _____

                                        _____

                                        _____

                                        _____

The benefits of this for both of us: _____

_____

_____

_____

'People with high levels of personal mastery [...] cannot
afford to choose between reason and intuition
or head or heart any more than they would choose
to walk with one leg or see with one eye.'
Peter Senge, author of The Fifth Discipline

Chapter 10

Working in a Team

Fulfillment – The Total View

My life is like a diamond
there for all to see
Cut with many facets
each shines a quality

For every face
that you can see
there is a different part of me

Love and happiness
are two sides
yet many others
prefer to hide

For those that take
the time to care
and stand back to know
what's really there

Fulfilment is the total view
a life of achievement
and trying things new.

By Melanie Theobald, reproduced with permission

This chapter focuses on working in teams. Many of us, whether in a job requiring high or low technical ability, rely on achieving results with and through other people, and positive emotion in teamwork is important. The activities at the end of the chapter provide scope for focusing on your actions as a member of a team, and for opening a dialogue on emotions.

A doctoral student, Cheryl Rice, has completed research recently on the relationship between individual team members' emotional intelligence and team performance.[i] She has uncovered that the role of emotional intelligence is a complex one. One of her key findings is that regulating emotions (managing emotions in one-self and in others) is of greater importance in team environments than is the ability to identify and understand emotions.[ii]

The following story demonstrates the importance of regulating emotion for one specific team.

Last year I was asked to coach a team that was dealing with a particularly difficult aspect of implementing government policy. They were a group of relatively new Team Leaders who were facing a difficult business objective. The Minister responsible for their area was very demanding and was expecting results quickly. When I first met them in spring last year, their meetings were highly disorganised and most team members didn't contribute – more than one person was trying to talk at once, there was a lot of frustration, there were new people who had just joined the team and who didn't seem to know what was happening. The team manager was oblivious to these undercurrents. One team leader was looking very harassed and his colleagues told me in confidence later that they thought he was heading for a breakdown, yet no one was saying this to him personally. They asked me what I could do for them. Looking back, I was aware that if I was going to help them make a difference, the difference would need to be tangible and also, it would need to happen relatively quickly. Here was a team that clearly would not survive unless it was able to manage its emotions within the group in order to influence positively the expectations of its key stakeholders outside the team (staff, the Minister, customers).

Seven months later, this team is quite different. I observed them recently at a meeting that brought together all parts of their division. It's clear that they have started to understand each other better. They have clear spokespeople – those team leaders who are better at communicating are the voice of the management team (and this is not necessarily the most senior person there). They laugh a lot, they see the lightness and the greatness in what they are doing, they're more able to give and receive praise.

This is an emotionally intelligent team in action, and the result of a deliberate sequence of activities, over a period of months, designed to help them confront issues and deal with them appropriately.

A study done by Robert Baron (1990) found that 'negative or critical feedback was considered a greater source of conflict and frustration than disputes over power, mistrust or personality struggles.'[iii] One of the keys to emotional intelligence for teams involves the ability to differentiate between validation and invalidation. Let's start by defining these words.

Validation means acknowledging, accepting, understanding and nurturing people and their feelings – it involves accepting someone's individuality. When the chips are down, very often all we need is to feel validated.

Invalidation is acting in a way that rejects, ignores, mocks, teases, judges, or diminishes someone, or someone's feelings. Invalidation goes beyond mere rejection, by implying not only that our feelings are disapproved of, but also that we are fundamentally abnormal. Invalidation is one of the most counterproductive ways to try to manage emotions. It kills confidence, creativity and individuality. Telling a person she shouldn't feel the way she does feel is akin to telling water it shouldn't be wet, grass it shouldn't be green, or rocks they shouldn't be hard. Each person's feelings are real. Whether or not we like or understand someone's feelings, they are still real. Rejecting feelings is rejecting reality; it is fighting nature and may be called a crime against nature, 'psychological murder', or 'soul murder'. So you can see why it's so frustrating, draining and futile.

In teams, particular forms of invalidation take place. It can sometimes involve keeping people in the dark about their performance, or using personal attacks, sarcasm, angry tones and the like. Such behaviour usually elicits one or more of these reactions: defensiveness, tension, antagonism, people making excuses or avoiding responsibility, people ignoring the leader and, ultimately, people leaving the organisation.

Activity 13: Validation and invalidation

This activity is inspired by Steve Hein's work on validation and invalidation in his work on families.

Think about how you are in the team that you work in. Put a tick next to all the items that are typical of you – if possible, check this out with a colleague.

VALIDATION		INVALIDATION
I accept, understand and nurture other people's feelings.		I tell others they shouldn't feel the way they feel.
I acknowledge and accept other people's unique identity and individuality.		I dictate to others not to feel the way they feel.
I allow other people to safely share their feelings and thoughts.		I tell others they are too sensitive and too 'dramatic'.
I reassure other people that I will still accept them even if they share their thoughts.		I ignore others.
I reassure others that it is okay to have the feelings they have.		I judge others.
I let other people know that I respect their perception of things.		I lead people to believe there is something wrong with them for feeling how they feel.
I help other people to feel heard, acknowledged, understood and accepted.		I reject people's individual identity.
I listen and show my agreement non-verbally (e.g. nods).		I am a poor listener – I have too much mental chat going on when I'm supposed to be listening to other people.
I am patient when others are not ready to talk.		I am impatient and often tap my hands and feet and fidget.
I offer to listen.		I don't often offer to listen to other people's views, particularly when feelings are involved.
I am present both physically and emotionally with other people.		I find it hard to stay in the present and stay focused on what someone is saying.
Total number of Validation		*Total number of Invalidation*

The next activity focuses on developing emotional intelligence in teams by focusing on creating a dialogue on emotions.

Activity 14: Team talk

The following list of questions, inspired by Steve Hein's work, is designed to provide dialogue on the emotional content of teamwork. Ask these questions of your team:

1. Have we started to talk about feelings?
2. Have we started to respect them?
3. Have we started to assign value to feelings?
4. Have we included feelings in our decision-making and problem resolution?
5. Have we been prepared to change track with a decision if it is creating negative emotion?
6. Have we listened to the most sensitive people in the organisation?
7. Have we struck a balance between emotion and logic?
8. Have we done our part in making our workplace somewhere where feelings are mutually respected?
9. Have we identified the key feelings that are important for success?
10. Have we established how we wish our employees and customers to feel in terms of their emotional experience of doing work/business?
11. Have we used other activities in this book to track feelings?

'The intimacy of work is like the intimacy of marriage.
Both involve vows.'
David Whyte

Chapter 11

Leadership

Werthers Original

Granddad?

Yes Son?

What does a passion do?

Well son, first of all, *it's* what is passion?

Passion is an excited feeling

or strong emotion

You remember I said about being in the war?

Yes

Well, I was passionate about protecting the country from Hitler

He was a nasty man you know

He too was passionate

He passionately believed that *his* people were the best in the world

And should rule the world

I got passionate about stopping his passion

Oh, I see

So a *passion* made Hitler want to rule the world and your passion helped stop him?

Yes, that's right

It was called World War 2

I've heard of a war, don't people get hurt and sometimes die?

Yes, quite

In fact the original meaning of passion is 'the suffering of pain'

From the suffering of Jesus on the Cross

I think I've heard of him

I'm sure you have, but that's another story

Now, would you like another sweetie?

By Neil Taylor, reproduced with permission

Much has been written on leadership and emotional intelligence. The world of business has been seduced with claims that you can increase someone's emotional intelligence and thereby affect the bottom line. I'm sure this is true, but what is of particular interest to me is the behaviour of someone who is emotionally intelligent in a leadership role. For me, the two things that set leaders apart are the extent to which they are open about themselves (and this reflects in the quality of the relationships that they develop both with peers and people who report to them) and the language that they use when trying to motivate people. It is these two aspects that are reflected within this chapter's activities.

A group of researchers have predicted that five main components are required in leaders of the future.[i] These are:

1. a knowledge-based technical speciality (e.g. chemistry, internet marketing)
2. cross-functional and international experience
3. collaborative leadership (leading a project team or being a team member)*
4. self-management skills (career planning and continuous learning)*
5. personal traits that include flexibility, integrity and trustworthiness.*

I believe that at least three of these, the ones marked with an asterisk, will require some emotional intelligence.

In Cheryl Rice's study on team leadership,[ii] she found a relationship between team leaders' emotional intelligence and team leaders' performance. Team leaders who were ranked highly as performers were also team leaders who scored high on every emotional intelligence sub-scale.[iii]

But what do excellent team leaders do in practice? This is my experience of what it feels like to work for excellent team leaders:

I used to work with a man called Martin who was my first boss and an excellent leader. He had an ability to sit down and listen, no matter what was happening. He treated everyone as if he was close to them. He was real, warm and empathetic. He was incredibly focused on the job in hand and business targets but, at the same time, he was generous with praise and was an honest person. He included everyone within his team – at the time, he was the only leader who called team meetings on a regular basis.

I have lost touch with Martin but he provided my early experience of what an emotionally intelligent leader is like to work with. I would have done anything for Martin – I would have followed him into battle.

A few years ago I met someone who had recently been chief executive of a company that had been losing market share. He had been asked to turn the company round, but once he had achieved this, he was asked to leave. Typically, he went somewhere else to do the same again. In terms of his physical self, he was larger than life, quite literally the largest man I have ever had a conversation with – he was excessively overweight and could barely squeeze into a chair. I found it hard to be in conversation with him – his sheer size was the only thing I could think about. I spoke to others who met him at the same time and they shared my sentiment. I believe he was quite unaware of the impact that his size had on the ability of others to listen to him. I started to understand how he had ended up in the kind of role he was doing – a bright man who had been asked to solve problems and then leave. He had different skills from the skills of a true leader, who brings other people with them and who develops longer-lasting relationships. Although I'm sure he has the potential to be a powerful leader, I can't help but think that he would need to get his weight under control before he could be totally powerful. He taught me the power of achieving despite obstacles but also the importance of being tuned into what is happening for people around you, and their reactions to the way we are. I can't help but wonder whether being more in shape might help him to be recruited on a more permanent basis.

The Center for Creative Leadership (in Greensboro, North Carolina, USA) studied the reasons for leaders losing track of their careers and found that it was never to do with cognitive ability – the two most common traits of those who failed were rigidity and poor relationships.[iv]

One of the first pieces of doctoral research on emotional intelligence has just been completed in the UK, at the Manchester School of Management, part of the University of Manchester Institute of Science and Technology. Mark Slaski studied the links between emotional intelligence, stress and performance. His study of 224 managers of a leading UK supermarket chain concluded that 'Managers higher in emotional intelligence suffer less stress, and enjoy better health, morale, quality of working life, and performance than managers with lower emotional intelligence.'[v] The implications of such studies is enormous – this particular study also concluded that it is possible to train managers in emotional intelligence so that they can manage other people both on an emotional level, and on a purely task-based level.[vi]

The following two activities are based on helping others know you and on developing more flexibility in how you deal with the emotional content of your leadership role.

Activity 15: Helping others to know you

Adapted from Discovering EQ *by Kate Cannon, Lisa Griebel, and Sue Stanek, used with permission.*

This activity is designed to make it easy for you to get to know the people you are leading. By being open about yourself, you free others to want to share their own background with you.

STEP 1: Write down the following information about yourself.
1. *Facts* – where you live, what you do for a living, your educational background, your family background, your hobbies.
2. *Values* – what is important to you in terms of family, friends, how you live your life?
3. *Vision, Dreams, Goals* – what are your important aspirations in life, both in work and in your personal life?

STEP 2: The next time you meet with your colleagues or your team, tell them this information.

STEP 3: *Invite others to do the same.* In a team, you might want to use a table like the one reprinted below to find out more about the other team members.

NAMES	FACTS Examples: where they live, what they do, educational background, family background, hobbies	VALUES What is important to this person in terms of family, friends, how they live their life?	VISION, DREAMS, GOALS What is important to this person in terms of their aspirations in life?

In order to succeed with Step 3, you will need to be very up-front about why you are asking people in your team to share this information. Tell them it is to make everyone aware of the backgrounds and experiences represented within the team.

Activity 16: Cost/benefit analysis

Two researchers[vii] have put forward a compelling argument for a relationship between transformational leadership and emotional intelligence (the former is broadly defined as the ability to understand and connect with those they lead emotionally so that their followers emotionally invest in their mission). Leaders need to have a clearer understanding of their emotions, understand others' emotions, regulate their own emotions, have skills in regulating others' emotions and be more competent in using emotional knowledge in decision-making.[viii]

This activity is designed for you as a leader to assess the key emotions both in yourself and in others, and your reactions under pressure.

STEP 1: ASSESSING KEY EMOTIONS

Ask yourself for three key words that reflect how you perceive yourself as a leader. Note them in the first column. Then identify how you *feel* about your leadership role and write this in the second column. Then identify the costs of these feelings about yourself – for you, for your role, for your health. Finally identify the benefits of these feelings.

Qualities: how I perceive myself	My feelings about my leadership role	Costs	Benefits
e.g. *Capable* *Intellectual* *Inspiring*	e.g. *happy, satisfied* e.g. *distressed, frustrated*	*I am not giving time to the rest of my life* *My health*	*I get what I want, I can influence people, people are motivated to do a good job*
Qualities: how others perceive me	**The feelings I create in others**	**Costs**	**Benefits**
e.g. *In control, solid*	e.g. *respect, fear*	*I am not as approachable as I could be*	*People listen to me*

STEP 2: REACTIONS UNDER STRESS

Now think about how you perceive yourself under stress. Go back over the lists and add any words that identify what happens when you are under pressure. It may be that the emotions you create are different ones – if so, add these. If they are the same, circle the ones that are particularly present.

STEP 3: COUNTERPRODUCTIVE EMOTIONS

Finally, identify the emotions that are most counterproductive for you, by circling the ones that have the highest costs.

'If one desires a change, one must be that change
before that change can take place.'
Gita Bellin

Chapter 12
Making Decisions

INNER PEACE

In peace
there are no more questions
only stillness

In peace
there are no pressures or demands
only calm

When I am peaceful
the roller coaster of life
becomes a circle

The choppiness of change
Becomes
whole again

In peace
my little voice inside
stops chatting all day

In peace, I am able to be with you
and far away from you

Because in peace
there is only love

Geetu Orme

So what does peace have to do with making decisions? Peace is about letting go and trusting that decisions based on our feelings are good decisions.

As we saw Chapter 2, all our decisions involve our emotions. This chapter is about helping you to tune into the emotions that are driving your decisions. The first of the two activities at the end will help you draw up a framework for creating the life you want, with a clear, day-to-day statement of how you wish to use your time. The second gives you a framework for analysing the emotions that you experience, particularly the ones that have the greatest consequences.

Eight years ago I was looking for a house, together with my then husband. We had drawn up a list of criteria – it needed to be this way and that way, and close to shops, and look a certain way. Then the estate agent called us about a house that was just coming onto the market. We went to see it reluctantly (it didn't meet three of our ten criteria). As soon as we walked in, we just knew it was the perfect house for us. So we put an offer in and moved in two months later.

A few years ago a friend of mine, Arnie, had a fund-raising day in aid of MENCAP, the mental health charity. His task was to raise £3,000 in one day. He invited fifty-five people and asked them to arrive at nine o'clock one Saturday morning. That day was one of the most enjoyable days I have ever spent. During the day, the people who had assembled were given a number of tasks to do; there was always an element of 'choice'. For instance, during the morning, he announced one of a series of 'practical tasks' and we were asked to group ourselves into three teams – an indoor team based at the house, an outdoor team and an indoor team based somewhere else. It was interesting how people immediately moved to one or other of the 'set' areas in the room. Later on, when I asked people what made them choose the team they did, everyone seemed to have created their own pictures and feelings of what it would be like and this is what they made their decision on, not on any known facts! It made me wonder whether 'whatever information we don't know, we make up'.

Sometimes decision-making is about trusting your gut feelings. How many times have you just had a feeling about something, and you went with your *heart* and it worked out? Sometimes when we go with our *head* it leads us to the wrong decisions.

I know a couple who decided to redo their bathroom a few years ago. They contacted a number of different bathroom companies and arranged for a consultant to visit them one evening from a specialist bathroom company. After being shown a number of bathroom designs and attractive fittings and tiles, Angela and Tony were confident that they would get a good deal. The consultant assured them their bathroom would be built by professionals and that they would throw in an electric shower, Jacuzzi, towels and champagne, all free of charge – but only if a decision was made on that night. At the time, Angela and Tony had the cash to pay for the whole bathroom in one lump sum but when the question of finance came up, the consultant suggested that they take out a five-year repayment plan which would cost more although they would have to pay nothing for the first six months. Even though the couple knew they had the cash, the option to have six months of credit seemed like a logical move. They felt persuaded to go along this route. However, at the same time they doubted the honesty of the consultant, but they managed to put this to one side. After they had signed on the dotted line, a whole string of disasters occurred – six months after completion of the bathroom the time came for paying the first instalment. This is when they discovered that the contract they had signed would cost them way more than they thought because the repayment included compounded interest. So a bathroom that should have cost them £5,000 was going to end up, with interest repayments, costing £14,000 over ten years – the salesperson had written 120 months' repayment instead of 60, and they hadn't noticed this. Angela and Tony ended up having to borrow money to pay for this bathroom early to avoid the excessive charges but they still paid double the original contract price. They have often 'kicked themselves' for not trusting a deeper sense of unease with the consultant.

One of the areas of decision-making that is largely in our control is how we use our time. The activities that follow are designed to tune you into what is important in your life.

Activity 17: Planting time

This activity was inspired by the work of Stephen Covey and by Doug Lennick of American Express who expressed the importance of our day-to-day actions reflecting what we believe is important.

One area that is particularly useful for decision-making is to be clear about how you want to spend your time. Using time well is a preventative strategy for making it easier to manage and deal with emotive situations as they arise. It also means that your weekly use of time reflects what you really want – I often hear people complain that they just don't spend enough time with their family or partner; others say they just don't have the time to do everything they want to do. This is an exercise that helps you to be very clear about how you use your time, and what is important to you. It will help you to deal with situations and make clear decisions as things arise. I have found that people who work through this activity sincerely are more likely to be able to maintain good relationships with others and live a life that is in tune with what they really want.

STEP 1: For each of the roles listed, identify what you really want in that part of your life, as a life goal. Use column 2. The goal can be very simple and short – for example to be fit and healthy, to be a caring and consistent friend, to be a great father, to do good work.

STEP 2: Then for each role, list the specific activities in a week that would provide evidence of this role being fulfilled. Use column 3. Make the activities really specific. For instance, if under 'Community' you wish to be a caring, consistent friend, you might phone your best friend a certain number of times each week; to be a great father may involve you doing certain activities with each of your children every weekend.

STEP 3: Then allocate a time per week to each role. Please note that all aspects to do with health will help – for example getting a minimum number of hours' sleep per night.

Role	Goal	Activities	Time allocation (total = 168 hours per week)
FAMILY			
HEALTH			
WORK			
COMMUNITY			
LEARNING AND GROWTH			
Total			168 hours

After working through this activity, Martin, who is in a management role, made this sign for his office:

Every week, I spend:

38 hours with my wife Janet
15 hours with my family

16 hours going out with friends
54 hours sleeping and keeping fit.

Therefore I have **35 hours** to come to work.

The next activity is designed to give you some practice in understanding where emotions come from and the decisions that we can make as a result.

We often have a choice between what is rational and what is irrational, and both of these paths have emotional and behavioural consequences. The psychologist Albert Ellis identified that every feeling has an activating *Event*, which creates rational or irrational *Beliefs and self talk* leading to *Consequences* which are emotional and behavioural. This is called EBC analysis.

Activity 18: EBC analysis

Complete the EBC analysis for five key emotions. You may wish to choose the ones that are particularly getting in your way.

For example, take the feeling of being *angry*.

Event – anger might be triggered by an event such as your partner criticising you.

Beliefs and self-talk – these are both rational and irrational. Examples of *irrational* beliefs and self-talk might be 'How dare he? He never seems to be happy with what I do.' *Rational* beliefs and self-talk might include, 'He has a point. I've not done my fair share of work in the house.'

Consequences – each belief and self-talk will have emotional or behavioural consequences. The irrational self-talk mentioned here ('How dare he?', etc.) may lead to anger or frustration, and the result (or behavioural consequence) is that I stop listening. The rational self-talk (e.g. 'He has a point', etc.) leads to only mild annoyance and results in greater listening.

Now complete an EBC analysis for some of the emotions that you identified in Activity 2 (Chapter 4). Select emotions that you would like to study and list, for each one, the Event, the Beliefs and self-talk (both rational and irrational) and the Consequences. You may wish to focus on the emotions that you identified as obstacles to your effectiveness.

Feeling 1: _____

Event	**Beliefs and self-talk**	**Consequences**
	(irrational)	→
	(rational)	→

Feeling 2: _____

Event	**Beliefs and self-talk**	**Consequences**
	(irrational)	→
	(rational)	→

Feeling 3: _____

Event	**Beliefs and self-talk**	**Consequences**
	(irrational)	→
	(rational)	→

Feeling 4: _____

Event	**Beliefs and self-talk**	**Consequences**
	(irrational)	→
	(rational)	→

Feeling 5: _____

Event	**Beliefs and self-talk**	**Consequences**
	(irrational)	→
	(rational)	→

Now look back over this list and circle the emotions that have the greatest consequences for how you live your life.

> 'This idea that decisions are made based on lots of
> rational facts is wrong – you take decisions based
> on 25 per cent of available facts.'
> *Martin Taylor, journalist and businessman*

Conclusion

We are at the beginning of a new focus on emotional intelligence. It is a privilege to be part of this shift of focus from what we are doing to how we are doing it, and I believe that the study of emotional intelligence offers a key set of skills to learn and to put into every curriculum, workplace and family.

At this point in time, there are many different definitions (see Appendix 1) and many different ways of living with emotional intelligence. I think this is a healthy search for the 'truth'. However, as Confucius said, 'If the names are not agreed upon, the dialogues will not be smooth.' This is certainly the position in the field at the moment, although I am hopeful that one model will soon emerge as the clear front-runner.

Dr. Reuven Bar-On summed it up nicely in his epilogue to the Technical Manual of the Emotional Quotient Inventory, and I would like to leave the last words to him:

> Although I do not know precisely how emotional intelligence will be defined in the end, I do know that it is part of general intelligence and can be measured along a continuum much like cognitive intelligence. It is an exciting experience for me to play a role in mapping out this new human territory.[i]

... You must learn one thing.
The world was made to be free in.

Give up all the other worlds
except the one to which you belong.
Sometimes it takes darkness and the sweet
confinement of your aloneness
to learn

anything or anyone
that does not bring you alive

is too small for you

David Whyte

Excerpt from 'Sweet Darkness', in *The House of Belonging*. Copyright 1996,
Many Rivers Press. Reproduced with permission.

Appendix 1
Definitions and Descriptions

/ˌdefɪˈnɪʃ(ə)n/ *n.*

1. *Emotional Intelligence (Definitions)*

All these definitions and descriptions were mentioned during sessions at a conference on emotional intelligence held in Chicago, October 2000, and during a conference on virtual reality that took place one month later in November 2000.

'Emotional intelligence is about using the power of emotion as a source of information, motivation and connection.'
Kate Cannon – creator of the world's first emotional intelligence programmes in American Express Financial Services

'Emotional intelligence is the practice of paying attention to one's own and other people's emotional states and using the information to inform one's actions.'
Liz Morris – Partner, Buckholdt Associates/Center for Applied Emotional Intelligence

'Emotional intelligence is the ability to sense, understand, and effectively apply the power of emotions as a source of energy, information, creativity, trust and connection.'
Esther Orioli – creator of the EQ Map

'Emotional intelligence is the ability to use your emotions to help you solve problems and live a more effective life. Emotional intelligence without intelligence, or intelligence without emotional intelligence, is only part of a solution. The complete solution is the head working with the heart.'
David Caruso – co-author, with John Mayer and Peter Salovey, of the MEIS/MSCEIT [i]

'Emotional intelligence is an array of emotional, personal and social abilities which influence one's overall ability to cope effectively with environmental demands and pressures.'
Dr. Reuven Bar-On – co-editor of The Handbook of Emotional Intelligence

2. *Emotional Intelligence (Descriptions)*

'Emotional intelligence involves the ability to read the unspoken feelings in individuals as well as the collective dynamic.'
David Ryback – author of Putting Emotional Intelligence to Work

'The development of emotional intelligence involves addressing the areas that are creating drag in your life, just as there is drag in planes when flying.'
Dr. Rich Handley – Head of Human Resources, Air Force Recruiting Service; organisation development consultant

'The key to emotional intelligence is to acknowledge that there is no separation between thinking and feeling – they are simultaneous activities. People who practise emotional intelligence are aware of the 'whole self – the head, heart *and* gut' of each person. Being emotionally intelligent requires personal self-awareness in the moments of interpersonal interactions.'
Faxon Green – Founder of Feeling Mind Institute

3. *Emotions and Feelings (Definitions)*

All these descriptions have been taken from the websites of Steve Hein and 6 seconds (see Appendix 5) during 2000 and 2001.

'Emotions are data, just like everything else. When we are not aware of them or try to manage them without understanding the data they provide, they unconsciously affect how we act – often with undesirable results. Many people are run by their emotions, even though they perceive themselves to be totally rational.'
Judith Orloff – President and CEO of Educational Discoveries, a company that focuses on Emotional Literacy

'An emotion occurs when there are certain biological, certain experiential, and certain cognitive states which all occur simultaneously. There are emotions, which are more biologically oriented, and then there are complex emotions that are saturated with thoughts and cognition.'
Dr. John Mayer – who, together with Dr. Peter Salovey, coined the term 'emotional intelligence'

'Emotions are human beings' warning systems as to what is really going on around them. Emotions are our most reliable indicators of how things are going in our lives. They are also like an internal gyroscope; emotions help keep us on the right track by making sure that we are led by more than cognition.'
Maurice Elias, PhD – co-author of Emotionally Intelligent
Parenting: Promoting Social and Emotional Learning, *and professor of education at Rutgers University*

'Emotions are the glue that holds the cells of the organism together in the material world, and in the spiritual world they're the glue that holds the classrooms and the society together. That's why they are so interesting, because they're on a material level – the molecules of emotion as I've studied them as a scientist – and they're in the spiritual realm as well.'
Candace Pert, PhD – author of Molecules of Emotion *and research professor at the Georgetown University Medical Center*

'Emotions are our responses to the world around us, and they are created by the combination of our thoughts, feelings, and actions. What is most important is for each of us to learn that we create our own emotions. Our responses are shaped by our beliefs – by what we tell ourselves. As we clarify our understanding of our own beliefs and patterns, we learn that we are actually choosing our own lives. We

take responsibility for our thoughts, feelings, and actions; we become accountable.'
Karen Stone McCown – Chairman and founder of Six Seconds, founder of the Nueva School, and co-author of Self Science

4. *Emotions and Feelings (Descriptions)*

'Emotions prioritise thinking by directing us to important information.'
John Mayer and Peter Salovey – from Emotional Development and Emotional Intelligence: Educational Implications, *p. 11*

'Stating your own feeling is being authentic and acts to encourage a like response from others.'
Peter Block – author of Flawless Consulting, *a highly acclaimed book on business consulting, p. 136*

'Emotions are cross-cultural – the same all over the world. Feelings are a subset of all of our mind-body states (disappointment, hunger, hope, etc. There are hundreds of them!). Feelings are a learned response in the culture in which you grow up (the family, the peers, the community, etc.).'
Eric Jensen, PhD – author of Brain-Based Learning, *director of Jensen Learning, and a co-founder of SuperCamp; online at www.thebrainstore.com*

'Emotions are generated in the brain and the brain drives the body. So I agree with Epictetus who stated, "We are disturbed not by things, but by the views we take of things." So first we think, then we feel, and then we act. And I think love, guilt, hate, happiness, anger – all the feeling-states – are byproducts of the actions we take. So love of a child comes from the exhilaration and excitement of the miracle of birth, plus the immeasurable hours of nurture, care, and service to his/her growth and development.

There are a hundred or perhaps a thousand other emotions, or gradations, created by the mixing, blending, and overlapping of the basic ones.

Emotions are the raw material. They come with the DNA package. Feelings are the interpretation of the raw data given by the brain and reinforced by the individual's culture.'
Anabel Jensen, PhD – President of Six Seconds, co-author of Self-Science *and* Handle With Care, *and professor of education at the College of Notre Dame, Belmont, California.*

'Emotions are partially or totally blocked actions. Who feels anxiety? The spectator watching or the player involved in the game? The student waiting to enter the exam or the student answering the exam? When you are not fully involved in action, the emotions will be noticeable and felt.

E-Motion is preparing and anticipating action. Feelings are the internal expression of the emotion and can be differentiated from body sensations and states: 'feeling cold' or 'feeling depressed'. The emotion 'behind' the feeling of depression: sadness or anger.'
Daniel Gil'Adi, PhD – professor in organisational management at Venezuela's IESA University and the director of the EQ development organisation Proyectos LEAD

---

[i] MEIS Feedback booklet, p. 3.

Appendix 2

Measurement Tools for Emotional Intelligence

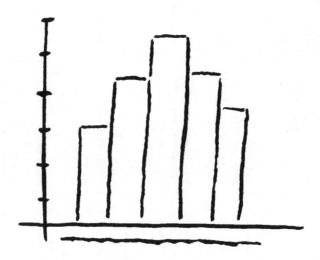

Within this section are listed the details of the main measures of emotional intelligence so that you and others can access them easily. See Chapter 3 and Appendix 3 for detailed descriptions of each of the tests mentioned here.

Ability	*Self Report*		*Multi-rater*		
Multifactor Emotional Intelligence Scale (MEIS) 1999 – Mayer, Salovey, Caruso & Chuck Wolfe Associates.	Bar-On EQ-i – Bar-On 1997 & Multi-Health Systems.	EQ Map™ – Cooper, 1996-7 & Q-Metrics.	Emotional Competence Inventory (ECI) – Boyatzis, Goleman & Hay McBer, 1999	Emotional intelligence Questionnaire (EIQ) – Higgs & Dulewicz & ASE – NFER-Nelson, 1999.	Ei-360– Institute of Health & Human Potential – IHHP, 2000
Emotional Perception Identifying emotions in faces, designs, music, stories	**Intrapersonal** Self regard, emotional self awareness, assertiveness, independence, self actualization	**Current Environment** Life pressures, life satisfactions	**Self Awareness** Emotional self awareness, accurate self assessment, self confidence	**Self Awareness**	**Self Awareness** Emotional self awareness, self assessment, self regard
Emotional Facilitation Translating feelings, using emotions to make judgments	**Interpersonal** Empathy, social responsibility, interpersonal relationship	**Emotional Literacy** Emotional self awareness, emotional expression, emotional awareness of others	**Social Awareness** Empathy, organisational awareness, service orientation	**Emotional resilience**	**Emotional management** Impulse control, living in alignment, adaptable/flexible, authenticity
Emotional Understanding Defining emotions, complex emotional blends, emotional transitions, emotional perspectives	**Adaptability** Reality testing, flexibility, problem solving	**EQ Competencies** Intentionality, creativity, resilience, interpersonal connections, constructive discontent	**Self Management** Self control, trustworthiness, conscientiousness, adaptability, achievement orientation, initiative	**Motivation** **Interpersonal sensitivity**	**Emotional connection** Empathy, communication, coaching others
Emotional Management Managing own emotions, managing others' emotions	**Stress Management** Stress tolerance, impulse control **General Mood** Happiness, optimism	**EQ Values and attitudes** Outlook, compassion, intuition, trust radius, personal power, integrated self **EQ Outcomes** General health, quality of life, relationship quotient, optimal performance.	**Social Skills** Developing others, leadership, influence, communication, change catalyst, conflict management, building bonds, teamwork	**Influence** **Intuitiveness** **Conscientiousness & Integrity**	**Personal leadership** Personal drive, optimism, self actualisation

continued

Multifactor Emotional Intelligence Scale (MEIS) 1999 – Mayer, Salovey, Caruso & Chuck Wolfe Associates.	Bar-On EQ-i – Bar-On 1997 & Multi-Health Systems.	EQ Map™ – Cooper, 1996–7 & Q-Metrics.	Emotional Competence Inventory (ECI) – Boyatzis, Goleman & Hay McBer, 1999	Emotional intelligence Questionnaire (EIQ) – Higgs & Dulewicz & ASE – NFER-Nelson, 1999.	Ei-360– Institute of Health & Human Potential – IHHP, 2000
Available from:					
Chuck Wolfe Associates Wolfe & Associates 59 Winterset Lane Simsbury CT 06070-1720 USA **Tel: +1-860-658-2737** **e-mail: cjwolfe@cjwolfe.com** **Web: www.cjwolfe.com**	**Multi-Health Systems 3770 Victoria Park Avenue Toronto ON M2H 3M6** **Tel: +1-800-268-6011 or +1-416-492-2627** **Fax: +1-888-540-4484 or +1-416-492-3343** **E-mail: customer_service @mhs.com** **Web: www.mhs.com** **See Appendix 5 for list of MHS international partners who train new users of the EQ-i.**	**Q-Metrics 70 Otis Street San Francisco California CA 94103** **Tel: +1-415-252-7557** **Fax: +1-415-252-5732** **E-mail: qmetricseq@aol.com** **Web: www.qmetricseq.com**	**In the UK:** **Hay Group Hay McBer 52 Grosvenor Gardens London SW1W 0AU** **Tel: +44-207-881-7000** **Fax: +44-207-881-7100** **In the US:** **Hay Group The Wanamaker Building 100 Penn Square East Philadelphia PA 19107-3388** **Tel: +1-215-861-2000** **Fax: +1-215-861-2111** **Web: www.ei.haygroup.com**	**ASE – Nfer Nelson Hanover House 2-4 Sheet Street Windsor Berkshire SL4 1BG** **Tel: +44-1753-850333** **Fax: +44-1753-620972** **E-mail: ase@ nfer-nelson.co.uk** **Web: www. ase-solutions.co.uk**	**IHHP – Institute for Health and Human Potential 143 Wyndham Street North Suite 203 Guelph Ontario N1H 4E9** **Tel: +1-519-836-0927** **Fax: +1-519-1039** **E-mail: inquiries@ihhp.com** **Web: www.ihhp.com**

Appendix 3

'Business' Schools of Emotional Intelligence

This appendix covers the three schools of:

1. The Emotional Competence Inventory (ECI) of Daniel Goleman
2. The Emotional Intelligence Questionnaire (EIQ) of Malcolm Higgs and Victor Dulewicz
3. The EQ Map of Q Metrics, founded by Esther Orioli and Robert Cooper.

As in Chapter 3, each school is introduced in the following way:

- who is behind each 'school'
- my view as a practitioner on the benefits and downsides of each measure[i]
- an overview of the school's definition and measure of emotional intelligence.

If you are making decisions on which measurement device to use for yourself, you will find that some of the business frameworks are riddled with what I call 'human resources-speak' – jargon that is not part of the language spoken day-to-day outside the world of large organisations and big training departments. However, these models do have value for people in the corporate world who prefer a purely work-focused measure of emotional intelligence.

1. The Emotional Competence Inventory (ECI)

Who is Behind It?

Daniel Goleman, who wrote the books *Emotional Intelligence* and *Working with Emotional Intelligence*, is now Chief Executive Officer of EI services of Hay McBer, a worldwide consulting firm that specialises in emotional intelligence measurement and development in large companies. Daniel Goleman authored the Emotional Competency Inventory (ECI) together with his colleague Richard Boyatzis.

Definition of Emotional Intelligence

Goleman and Boyatzis define emotional intelligence as the 'capacity for recognising our own feelings and those of others, for motivating ourselves, and for managing emotions well in ourselves and in our relationships.'[ii]

Benefits of the ECI

1. Based on research over a period of thirty-five years in large organisations.
2. Can be used for coaching and development.
3. There is validation data within each report, confirming the level of agreement between different people who rated you and their familiarity with you.
4. It can be customised to suit a particular organisation or sector, using data collected either from within the organisation or from a similar job sector.

Downsides of the ECI

1. The data is based on leaders in mainly large companies[iii] – this may not necessarily be representative of fields other than in the world of business. Also, if the stars of the future have yet to be spotted, then this data by definition may be incomplete.
2. It tends to be more favoured by senior managers but many organisations already have 360-degree measures of effectiveness.
3. The test was based on an earlier test called the Self-Assessment Questionnaire, by Richard Boyatzis.[iv]
4. The list of competences is very long – twenty in total, under four categories. See Appendix 2.
5. Some of the groupings are unclear and there are many similar categories.
6. Expensive and cumbersome to administer as other people are required.
7. Not suitable for use in recruitment as it is not appropriate to involve other people (e.g. your peers) in assessing your emotional intelligence when you are going for your next job.
8. Whilst Daniel Goleman's model stresses the Mayer–Salovey approach, his competences bear little resemblance to their definition (see Chapter 3). They are a mixture with a corporate bias.
9. The concept of 'tipping point' is used – in other words, the point at which you tip into 'star' performance. But if you are doing the test for yourself only (as opposed to part of an organisation-wide scoring) the data will not exist to calculate this score for you. Where it is calculated, you may find that the chosen 'tipping point' is not relevant to your own skills and job demands.
10. When other people are involved, there is a view that they are rating a person's reputation (e.g. are they known for being a good listener) rather than how they actually are.[v]
11. This measure is purely work-based and contains much 'corporate-speak' that may not be meaningful to people in a variety of jobs.
12. Recent UK research in a secondary school suggests that there can be a limited tendency of those in authority roles to spot the talented 'stars'.[vi] This throws the value of a multi-rater test into doubt, particularly in organisations where there is a suspected 'hidden agenda' or low trust in work relationships.

What Does it Measure, and How?

The ECI is a questionnaire that you and up to fifteen other people complete, rating your emotional intelligence. There are 110 statements, and you and others are asked to give ratings on a seven-point scale ranging from 'slightly' to 'very'.

The ECI measures the following components:

- self-awareness
- self-management
- social awareness
- social skills.

More detail on what is included can be found in Appendix 3.

Final Word

Measures leadership competences, rather than emotional intelligence. Useful only for people in large corporations, who understand the jargon.

2. The Emotional Intelligence Questionnaire (EIQ)

Who is Behind It?

Drs. Malcolm Higgs and Victor Dulewicz of Henley Management College are two professors who have been doing their own research into emotional intelligence. During a UK summit on Emotional Intelligence in May 2000 they unveiled their view of it. Their test is marketed by ASE – a division of NFER-Nelson, a UK test publisher.

Definition of Emotional Intelligence

Higgs and Dulewicz define emotional intelligence as: 'Achieving one's goals through the ability to manage one's own feelings and emotions, to be sensitive to and influence other key people and to balance one's motives and drives with conscientious and ethical behaviour.'[vii]

Benefits of the EIQ

1. There are now four versions available, including a self-report for managers, a 'general' self-report for non-managers, a 360-degree review for managers and a 'general' 360-degree review.
2. Attractive packaging with dolphin branding.

Downsides of the EIQ

1. Simplistic compared to all other models that have been researched and used with thousands of people.
2. I have the impression that this test was marketed before it was fully developed. Anecdotally, users of the instrument have indicated that many people score 'similarly'.
3. Questionnaire looks superficial and is purely work-related.
4. Testing a narrow population of people – management students at Henley Management College created data that underpins the instrument and so it lends itself mainly to management development. Others will find less use for the instrument.
5. The reports that are produced are superficial and therefore of limited use.
6. The model and the descriptions are still changing. For example, Intuitiveness is a new term – it changed from Decisiveness early in 2000.

What does the EIQ Measure, and How?

There are sixty-nine items on the questionnaire, which you are asked to score on a five-point scale from 'never' to 'always'. It takes thirty minutes to complete and measures the following components:

- self-awareness
- emotional resilience
- motivation
- interpersonal sensitivity
- influence
- intuitiveness
- conscientiousness & integrity.

Final Word

Very superficial; needs more research to make it a valid and reliable measure.

3. The EQ Map

Who is Behind It?

Esther Orioli, who specialises in emotional intelligence pro-grammes, created the EQ Map, which is a measure of emotional intelligence for leadership and business. An early version of the map was published in Robert Cooper and Ayman Sayaf's book *Executive EQ: Emotional Intelligence in Leadership*. Dr. Cooper and Esther Orioli are the founders of Q Metrics – a company dedicated to measuring and developing human intelligence at work.

Definition of Emotional Intelligence

Page 1 of the EQ Map gives the following definition: 'Emotional intelligence is the ability to sense, understand and effectively apply the power and acumen of emotions as a source of human energy, information and influence.'

Benefits of the EQ Map

1. The EQ Map has been tested with over 2,500 executives, professionals and employees throughout the United States and Canada.
2. It is easy to administer – there is a booklet containing the statements and people score it themselves.
3. Comes in a neat pack including a questionnaire, scoring grid, interpretation guide and action planning worksheets.
4. The term 'Map' creates a useful impression when people are completing it.
5. High-quality, well-packaged glossy materials.
6. Extensively researched, norm-tested, statistically reliable and cross-validated.
7. Has some questions that act as 'lie detectors'.
8. Users have defined it as a 'unique, non-judgemental, interactive approach'.[viii]

Downsides of the EQ Map

1. There are a large number of different scales – too many to manage.
2. Designed mainly for the business population.
3. Describes four performance zones using the words *optimal, proficient, vulnerable, caution* – the use of the latter two words requires a high level of sensitivity in coaching situations.

What does the EQ MAP Measure, and How?

It is designed for individuals to assess their Emotional Quotient levels and improve their EQ leadership and performance at work. By transferring scores to the 'map', it is possible to pinpoint strengths and 'vulnerabilities'. The EQ Map measures twenty scales grouped into five main factors:

- current environment
- emotional literacy
- EQ competencies
- EQ values and attitudes
- EQ outcomes.

See Appendix 2 for descriptions of what is contained in each of these five scales.

Final Word

Useful as a self-scoring device. Too many EQ factors to take into account.

---

[i] The word 'measure' is used to refer to the questionnaire or test or instrument for measuring emotional intelligence.

[ii] Boyatzis, R.E., Goleman, D & Hay/McBer (1999) – p. 1

[iii] Some data on headteachers has just been published; however, most of the data from the Hay Group on Emotional Competence is from multinational companies around the world.

[iv] Presentation by Richard Boyatzis on the ECI during Linkage Conference, September 1999.

[v] Mayer, Caruso, Salovey (in press) – p. 6

[vi] Dissertation completed by Ian Gasson as part of a Masters in Education. Unpublished.

[vii] By Dulewicz & Higgs, 1999 – quoted in ASE presentation on the Ei Questionnaire – 1999.

[viii] Buckholdt Associates website, December 2000.

Appendix 4

List of Recommended Organisations Specialising in Emotional Intelligence

The following people and organisations are ones that I have worked with, either directly or on joint projects. Most are specialists in emotional intelligence programmes. Additional resources are listed in Appendices 5 and 6.

1. In the USA

The **Institute of HeartMath** is a not-for-profit research and training organisation which has developed simple, user-friendly tools that can be used to relieve stress, enhance health, change behaviour and improve performance in children and adults. Through innovative research and public education, they aim to facilitate more balance and health in people's lives by (1) researching the effects of positive emotions on physiology, quality of life, and performance; (2) helping individuals engage their hearts to transform stress and rejuvenate their health; and (3) providing prevention and intervention strategies for improved emotional health, decision-making, learning skills and violence reduction in families, schools and communities. Their website is at www.heartmath.com

The **Consortium for Research on Emotional Intelligence in Organizations (Ei Consortium)** conducts research into emotional intelligence and publishes guidelines for developing emotional intelligence; it is open to corporate membership for employers and others (details from Cary Cherniss, e-mail: cherniss@rci.rutgers.edu). Its website is a general source of information on emotional intelligence and, while the consortium 'does not evaluate or endorse measures', it provides background information on four emotional intelligence questionnaires. It has developed best-practice guidelines on the process of developing emotional intelligence among employees and managers. The website is at www.eiconsortium.org

The **EQ Network** is a 'virtual organisation' of professionals who help individuals and organisations leverage the power of emotion. Members of the network offer assessment, coaching and training programmes. The Network was founded in 1999 by Kate Cannon, who is recognised as a pioneer in the implementation of emotional intelligence programmes. She developed an award-winning emotional intelligence programme at American Express in the early 1990s and is now an independent emotional intelligence consultant and trainer. Kate can be contacted at: katecannon@earthlink.net; *Tel:* +1 952 929 0225

David R. Caruso, PhD, is a management psychologist. David provides consulting services to organisations in the areas of leadership and career development. He conducts in-depth assessments, coaching, workshops and seminars. As a co-developer of the Multifactor Emotional Intelligence Scale (MEIS), David is also in the forefront of work on emotional intelligence assessment and training. He can be contacted at: Work-Life Strategies, 112 Adams Lane, New Canaan, CT 06840, USA; *Tel:* +1 203 966 7980; *E-mail:* davidcaruso@worklife.com; *Website:* www.emotionalIQ.com

Six Seconds is a charity concerned with emotional intelligence, providing training, and publishing information and details of conferences and workshops. It has developed its own model of emotional intelligence and has published a number of useful resources for teachers and parents. The charity has an annual conference which brings together key practitioners in the field. Contact: Six Seconds, 316 Seville Way, San Mateo, CA 94402, USA;

Tel: +1 650 685 9885; *Fax:* +1 650 685 9880; *E-mail:* josh@6seconds.org
Website: www.6seconds.org

Gang & Gang, Inc. is a company which provides consulting and market/organisation research insights to major companies. It developed and commercialised Resonance, a proprietary research technique that elicits and quantifies emotions connected with any stimulus, including specific products, services, jobs, brands, advertising, memories and the future. They can be contacted at: 16 Front Street, Salem, MA 01970, USA; *Tel:* +1 978 740 4474; *Fax:* +1 978 744 8808; *E-mail:* thegang@gang.net; *Website:* www.gang.net

Chuck Wolfe Associates is a professional consulting firm with clients in the top 100 Fortune companies. Their expertise is in the area of applied emotional intelligence to culture change, team development, management development and employee development. Headed by Charles J. Wolfe. Contact: Chuck Wolfe Associates, 59 Winterset Lane, Simsbury, CT 06070-1720, USA. *Tel:* +1 860 658 2737; *E-mail:* cjwolfe@cjwolfe.com; *Website:* www.cjwolfe.com

2. In Canada

The Institute for Health and Human Potential (IHHP) is a consultancy that trains individuals and organisations in emotional intelligence; it has developed the EI 360 assessment tool. Dr J. P. Pawliw-Fry is co-director of IHHP.com and author of *You Can't Stop the Waves But You Can Learn to Surf: A Path to Emotional Intelligence*. The IHHP specialises in designing and delivering programmes in EI for leaders, managers, sales teams and Olympic and elite athletes. IHHP.com has developed the first train-the-trainer programme that integrates a state-of-the-art, web-enabled 360-degree EI assessment with experiential learning. Contact: IHHP – Institute for Health & Human Potential, 143–203 Wyndham Street North, Suite 203, Guelph, Ontario N1H 439, Canada; *Tel:* +1 519 836 0927; *Toll free:* 1877 264 4447; *Fax:* +1 519 767-0698; *E-mail:* inquiries@ihhp.com or JP@ihhp.com; *Website:* www.jp@ihhp.com

Multi-Health Systems is the test publisher that owns the world-wide distribution rights to the Bar-On Emotional Quotient Inventory (EQ-i) and the Mayer, Salovey, Caruso Emotional Intelligence Test (MSCEIT). They will be able to put you in touch with their representatives in different countries around the world. Contact: Multi-Health Systems, 3770 Victoria Park Avenue, Toronto, ON M2H 3M6, Canada; *Tel:* +1 800 268 6011 or +1 416 492 2627; *Fax:* +1 888 540 4484 or +1 416 492 3343; *E-mail:* customerservice@mhs.com; *Website:* www.mhs.com

Sagacity – Lea Brovedani has designed and implemented emotional intelligence training programmes in both schools and business. Lea is qualified in the use of the Bar-On EQ-i. She can be contacted at: +1 902 835 1623; *E-mail:* lbrovedani@sagacityeq.com; *Website:* www.sagacityeq.com

3. In Europe

Ei (UK) Limited is one of Europe's first companies to be dedicated to the assessment and development of emotional intelligence. Geetu Orme is the Managing Director. Ei (UK) Limited has developed unique and innovative programmes including public courses, team programmes, personal coaching and accrediting trainers to use our programmes. General information can be found at www.eiuk.com. For information about our programmes, contact Ei (UK) Limited, Monks Heath Hall Workshops, Chelford Road, Nether Alderley, Cheshire, UK; *Tel:* +44 (0)1625 890 220; *Fax:* +44 (0)1625 890 240; *E-mail:* geetu@eiuk.com; *Website:* www.eiuk.com

Hunter Kane Resource Management is a UK consultancy which owns the European distribution rights to the Institute of HeartMath's materials, including IQM. They own the European Union rights to the Inner Quality Management Programme. Their workshops in the corporate sector have created a set of research results showing improvements in personal productivity sustained over six months. They can be contacted at 26 Broad Street, Wokingham, Berkshire RG40 1AB, UK; *Tel:* +44 (0)118 989 0101; *Fax:* +44 (0)118 989 2333; *E-mail:* office@hunterkane.com

Kandidata Online Search AB is a Stockholm-based consultancy headed by Dr. Margareta Sjölund. It offers a wide range of human resources consulting and testing services, including the use of the Bar-On EQ-i. Their tests are used for recruiting, evaluation, strategic planning, skills and personnel development, and organizational development. Contact: Kandidata Online Search AB, Banérgatan 37, 2tr, PO Box 10158, S-100 55 Stockholm, Sweden; *Tel:* +46 8 545 85 010; *Fax:* +46 8 545 85 019; *E-mail:* info@kandidata.se; *Website:* www.kandidata.se

Dr. Reuven Bar-On coined the term 'EQ', developed the first test of emotional intelligence (the EQ-i) and edited the first textbook on this topic (*The Handbook of Emotional Intelligence*). He is presently being appointed to Conjunct Professor at Trent University in Canada, where he will co-direct the Emotional Intelligence Research Laboratory together with James Parker. Dr. Bar-On is a member of the Collaborative to Advance Social and Emotional Learning at the University of Illinois and a member of the Consortium for Research on Emotional Intelligence in Organizations at Rutgers University in the US. Together with James Parker, he has also co-authored the first test of emotional intelligence for children and adolescents (the EQ-i:YV). Based on a training manual he co-authored with Rich Handley (*Optimizing People*), he developed an e-learning programme for EQ University designed to improve emotional and social competence. Together with Dr. Handley, he also co-developed the EQ-Interview and EQ-360, two additional tools that assess emotional and social competence. Dr. Bar-On, together with Claus Moller in Denmark, recently began developing a model and measure of 'organisational emotional intelligence'. Reuven Bar-On can be contacted directly at rebaron@attglobal.net

Appendix 5

Internet Sites of Other Organisations

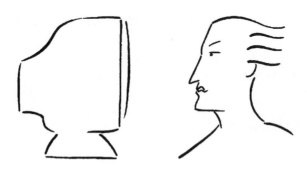

This list gives sources of information in addition to those listed in Appendices 3 and 4.

1. Useful Up-to-date Information on What is Happening in the World of EQ

EI World: www.eiworld.org
The EQ Network: www.eqnetwork.org
EQ Institute (Steve Hein): www.eqi.org

2. School/Education

6 Seconds EQ directory for schools:
    www.eq.org/K12-Schools/Resources
CASEL (Center for Applied Social and Effective Learning):
    www.casel.org
College of Life: www.collegeoflife.org

Educators for social responsibility/Resolving Conflict Creatively
    Program (RCCP): www.esrnational.org; www.rccp.org;
    www.triune.ca/rcc.htm
Michelle Seligson's after school programmes:
    www.bringyourselftowork.com
Online teacher development:
    www.thirteen.org/wnetschool/concept2class/index.html
Tom Snyder: www.tomsnyder.com

3. Other Good 'Causes' and Initiatives

EQ Parenting: www.eqparenting.com
Antidote: www.antidote.org.uk

4. Consultants

@ Key: www.atkey.co.uk
Aja 4 HR: www.aja4hr.co.uk
Atticus: www.atticus.co.uk
Centre for Applied Emotional intelligence: www.eicentre.com
Consultation Ltd.: www.consultation.ltd.uk
Corporate Vitality: www.corporate-vitality.co.uk
Educational Discoveries Inc.: www.ediscoveriesinc.com
Ei (UK) Limited: www.eiuk.com
Feeling Mind Institute: www.feelingmind.com
Fenman: www.fenman.co.uk
Grand Shearman: www.grand-shearman.com
Heartskills: www.heartskillscoach.com
HR Team: www.hrteam.co.uk
Human Assets: www.humanassets.co.uk
Integra Learning Systems: www.integralearning.com
Leaders in Sync Inc.: www.faithralston.com
Learn to Learn: www.learntolearn.co.uk
Mason Headway: www.mason-headway.co.uk
Michelle Seligson: www.bringyourselftowork.com
People Systems Potential: www.peoplesystemspotential.com
Peter Feltham: www.intelligentorgs.com
Quorum Training: www.quorumtraining.co.uk
Rheingold Associates: www.rheingold.com

Talent foundation: www.talentfoundation.org
The fine art of feelings: www.thefineartoffeelings.com
The Success Group: www.thesuccessgroupintl.com
Uncommon Knowledge: www.uncommon-knowledge.co.uk
Work Ecology: www.workecology.com
Youniverse b.v.b.a.: www.2youniverse.com
Youniverse s.p.r.l: www.emotelligence.com

5. Organisations Licensed to Train Other People in the Bar-On EQ-i

David Cory, Canada: www.davidcory.com
Ei (UK) Limited, England: www.eiuk.com
PEN Psychodiagnostics, The Netherlands: www.psyline.nl
Kandidata, Sweden: www.kandidata.se
Jopie Van Rooyen & Partners, South Africa:
    www.vanrooyen.co.za
MGT Consultoria, Mexico: www.infosel.net.mx

6. To Source Books on Emotional Intelligence (see Bibliography)

Crown House Publishing: www.crownhouse.co.uk
7 Lessons in Emotional Intelligence follow link from: www.7eq.com
Handbook of Emotional Intelligence follow link from:
    www.eiconsortium.org
Amazon: www.amazon.com or www.amazon.co.uk
Winslow Press (stories for troubled children):
    www.winslow-press.co.uk

7. Web-based Emotional Intelligence Programmes

Addeq: www.addeq.com
EQ university: www.equniversity.com

8. On-line Measures of Emotional Intelligence

On-line emotional intelligence test: www.utne.com/azEq2.tmpl
Test Agency, UK: www.thetestagency.com
CIM Publishers: www.cimtp.com

9. On Emotions, the Brain and Health
(in addition to the resources listed in Appendix 2)

Reuters Health: www.reutershealth.com
Plain Health: www.plainhealth.com
Brainwaves Centre: www.mentalmuscles.com
Layperson's description of brain and chemicals:
www.maui.net/~jms/brainuse.html
Work ecology stories on health: www.storiesofhealth.com
Geneva emotion research group: www.unige.ch/fapse/emotion

Appendix 6

Audio-visual and Other Resources

1. Multi-media

EQ Toolkits 1, 2 & 3 – Geetu Orme, Ei (UK) Limited.
A full resource for trainers, change agents and consultants, to design and implement an emotional intelligence programme. Includes tried-and-tested activities, processes and information. Available for use in training, coaching, self-development and awareness-raising. Call for current details of toolkit and licensing options. *Tel:* +44 (0)1625 890 220; *Fax:* +44 (0)1625 890 240; *E-mail:* eqtoolkit@eiuk.com; *Website:* www.eiuk.com

Many Rivers Company – David Whyte Materials.
Tapes, poetry books and videotape recordings of live talks by David Whyte, poet, distributed by Many Rivers Company, P.O. Box 868, Langley, WA 98260, USA. *Tel:* +1 360 221 1324; *Fax:* +1 360 221 6212; *E-mail:* mrivers@whidbey.com; *Website:* www.davidwhyte.com

2. Software

CD-ROM *From Chaos to Coherence* – Institute of HeartMath. Essential know-how on HeartMath tools and techniques. Includes 100 minutes of video segments. Available through Planetary Publications, P.O. Box 66, 14700 West Park Avenue, Boulder Creek, CA 95006 USA; *Tel:* +1 800 372 3100 or +1 408 338 2161. Planetary Publications is affiliated to The Institute of HeartMath (same address as Planetary Publications). *Tel:* +1 800 450 9111 or +1 831 338-9700; *Fax:* +1 831 338 9861; *Website:* www.heartmath.com

Freeze-Framer™ **Emotional Management Enhancer**
Software which displays your physiological state by recording your heart rhythms through a fingertip pulse sensor that plugs into the serial port of your computer. Includes Freeze-Frame book and user's manual. Available through Institute of HeartMath (see above for details).

3. Video

Daniel Goleman video
Emotional Intelligence – a 90-minute video, with book, distributed by Producers Media International. Available from Video Arts Group, Dumbarton House, 68 Oxford Street, London W1N 0LH, UK. *Tel:* +44 (0)207 637 7288; *Fax:* +44 (0)207 580 8103; *E-mail:* enquiries@videoarts.co.uk; *Website:* www.videoarts.co.uk

The George Lucas Educational Foundation has video interviews on the internet with Dr. Goleman and other experts on education – www.glef.org/eigallery.html. In an exclusive article, Goleman reflects on advances made since his 1995 book. The article can be accessed directly at www.glef.org/fiveyears.html

4. Audio-cassettes and CDs

Nathaniel Branden
Honoring the self and other cassettes available through:
www.nathanielbranden.net/boobi.shtml

Daniel Goleman
Abridged version of *Emotional Intelligence* on audio-cassette –
approximate duration: three hours. Produced by Audio
Renaissance Tapes, division of Cassette Productions Unlimited,
Inc., 5858 Wiltshire Boulevard, Suite 205, Los Angeles, CA 90036,
USA. Available through www.amazon.com or
www.amazon.co.uk

Heartzones
CD containing 17 minutes of specially designed music, to
practice Heart Lock-in®, one of the Institute of HeartMath's
techniques for generating coherence. Available through the
Institute of HeartMath (see above for details).

You Can't Stop The Waves But You Can Learn To Surf
A four-cassette audio programme on emotional intelligence by
Dr. J. P. Pawliw-Fry. Includes exercises on mindfulness. Available
through IHHP (see above for details).

Mindfulness Meditation
Audio-cassettes recorded by Jon Kabat-Zinn, PhD, the founder
and former director of the Stress Reduction Clinic at the
University of Massachusetts Medical Center. He is the executive
director of the Center for Mindfulness in Medicine, Health Care,
and Society. Details of his mindfulness tapes can be found at
www.mindfulnesstapes.com. His e-mail address is
jonkabat-zinn@umassmed.edu

5. *Journal*

Competency and Emotional Intelligence
The only journal of its kind in Europe, with a section dedicated
to emotional intelligence – business-focused and practical, not
theoretical. Includes articles from leading emotional intelligence
practitioners including a series of four articles published in
2000–01 entitled 'How to Get Started with an EQ Initiative'.
Published by IRS, 18–20 Highbury Place, London N5 1QP, UK;
Tel: +44 (0)20 7354 6747; *Fax:* +44 (0)20 7354 8106;
Website: www.irs-eclipse.com. Editor: Neil Rankin,
E-mail: neil.rankin@butterworths.com

6. For Children

EQ Coaching for Kids
A two-cassette audio programme by Dr. J. P. Pawliw-Fry, aimed at parents. Available through the Institute for Health and Human Potential (IHHP), 143 Wyndham Street North, Suite 203, Guelph, Ontario N1H 4E9, Canada; *Tel:* +1 519 836 0927; *Fax:* +1 519 836 1039; *E-mail:* inquiries@ihhp.com; *Website:* www.ihhp.com

Emotionally Intelligent Dolls
'Peaches' and 'Babin' are hand-made in Toronto and are sold through mail order by Dr. Pearson's Wonderful Toy Company, Inc., 27 Wendover Road, Toronto M8X 2L1, Canada; *Tel:* +1 416 233 7776; *Fax:* +1 416 236 9777; *Website:* www.wondertoy.com

Educators for Social Responsibility
'Socially responsible' toys. *Website:* www.peacetoys.com

Appendix 7

Feelings Words List

This list was compiled by Steve Hein, an independent researcher and consultant. Thank you to Steve for permission to reproduce his list.

A

abashed abandoned abhorred abnormal absent-minded absolved absorbed abused accelerated accepted acclaimed acclimated accommodated accommodating accomplished accountable accused acknowledged acquiescent acquisitive active actualised addicted admired adored adrift advanced affable affected affectionate affluent afraid affronted agoraphobic aggravated aggressive agitated agony alarmed alert alienated alive alone aloof allied allured alluring altruistic amazed ambiguous ambivalent amenable amiable ambushed amused analysed angry anguish annihilated anonymous annoyed antagonistic anticipation antiquated antisocial antsy anxiety anxious apathetic appalled appealed appealing appeased applauded apologetic appraised appreciated appreciative apprehensive appropriate approved of ardent argumentative artificial artful artistic artless aroused ashamed asinine assaulted astonished astounded at ease at home at peace at war attached attacked attracted attractive audacious authentic available avaricious avoided awakened aware awe awesome awe-struck awkward

B

babied bad badgered baffled baited balanced bamboozled banished bankrupt bantered barraged bashful beaten beaten down beckoned bedevilled befriended befuddled beholden belittled belligerent bemused benevolent berated bereaved bereft beseeched besieged betrayed bewitched bewildered bitter blackmailed blamed blasé blasphemous blasted blind blithe blocked blown away blue bogus bold bombastic bored bothered bothersome brainwashed brave bridled brilliant broken brutal bugged bummed burdened burdensome buried burned out bypassed

C

caged callous callow calm cantankerous capable cared about cared for carefree careless caring capricious categorised captivated captured caught cautious cavalier censored centred certain chafed chagrined challenged charismatic charitable charmed chaste chastised cheap cheated cheated on cheerful cherished chided childish childlike chipper choked-up churlish circumspect circumvented civil civilised claustrophobic clean cleansed clear clever close closed clueless clumsy coddled coerced cold cold-blooded cold-hearted collected combative comfortable committed common comparative compared compassionate compatible competent competitive complacent complete complicated compliant composed compulsive conceited concerned condemned considerate considered confident confined confused congenial connected conned conquered considerate consistent conspicuous constrained constructive contained contemplative contempt content contented contentious contrite controlled conventional convicted cordial cornered corrupt counterfeit courageous courteous cowardly cultivated crabby cranky craving crazed crazy creative crestfallen crippled critical criticised cross cross-examined crowded cruel crushed curious cursed cynical

D

damned daring dashed daunted dazed dead debased debauched debilitated deceitful deceived decimated dedicated defamed defeated defective defenceless defensive deferent defiant deficient defiled definite deflated degraded dehumanised dejected delicate delighted demanding demented demoralised demure denatured denigrated denurtured dependent depleted depraved depressed deprived derided derailed desecrated deserted deserving desirable desired despair desperate despised despondent destroyed destructive detached determined detest detested devastated deviant devious devoted devoured diagnosed different difficult diffident diligent diminished directionless dirty disaffected disappointed disapproving disapproved of disbelieved disbelieving discarded discombobulated disconcerted disconnected discontent discontented discounted discouraged discredited disdainful dissected disgraced disgruntled disgusted disheartened dishevelled dishonest dishonourable dishonoured disillusioned disinclined disingenuous disinterested disjointed dislodged disloyal dismal dismayed dismissed disobedient disobeyed disowned disorganised disoriented disparaged dispassionate dispensable displaced displeased disposable dispossessed disregarded disrespected disruptive dissatisfied distant distorted distracted distraught distressed distrusted distrustful disturbed diverted divorced docile doomed double-crossed doubtful drained dramatic drawn in driven dropped drubbed dubious dull dumb dumbfounded dumped dumped on duped

E

eager early easy-going ebullient ecstatic edgy educated effaced effective effervescent efficacious egotistical elastic elated elevated elusive emancipated emasculated embarrassed empathetic emphatic emotional empowered empty enchanted encouraged encumbered endangered energetic energised enervated engaged engrossed enhanced enlightened enmeshed enraged enriched entangled entertained enthralled enthusiastic enticed entrapped entrusted envious eradicated erasable erased esteemed established estranged euphoric evaluated evaded evasive evicted evil exacerbated examined exasperated excellent excited excluded excoriated exempt exhausted exhilarated exiled exonerated exorcised expectant exploitative exploited explosive exposed expressive extravagant extraordinary exultant exuberant

F

faithful fake fallible false fanatical fanciful fantastic fatalistic fathered fatherless fatigued fatuous favoured fearful fearless fed up feisty felicitous fervent fickle fidgety fine finished fit flabbergasted flammable flappable flat flawed fleeced flighty flush flustered focussed foiled followed fond foolhardy foolish forgettable forgetful forgiven forgiving forgotten formidable forsaken fortunate fractured fragile fragmented frail framed frantic fraudulent free frenetic fresh fretful frenzied friendly frightened frisky frivolous frolicsome frustrated fulfilled full funny furious fussy

G

galled gauche generous gentle giddy gifted giving glad gleeful gloomy glorious glowing glum goaded good gorgeous graded grateful great greedy gregarious grief grief-stricken grieved grieving gross grossed-out grotesque grouchy grumpy guarded guilt-free guiltless guilty gullible gushy gutsy gypped

H

hampered handicapped happy harnessed harangued harried hassled hate hated hateful hatred haunted healed healthy heard heartbroken heartful heartened helped helpful helpless herded hesitant high-spirited hindered hollow honourable honoured hoodwinked hopeful hopeless horrible horrified hospitable hostile hounded humble humiliated hurt hyper hyperactive hypocritical hysterical

I

idealistic idiotic idolised ignorant ignored imaginative imbalanced immature immobilised immodest immune impaired impartial impassioned impassive impatient impeded impelled imperilled imperfect impertinent imperturbable impervious implacable important imposed upon impressed imprisoned impudent impugned impulsive impure in control in the way in touch in tune inadequate inappropriate inattentive inauthentic incensed incompetent incomplete inconsiderate inconspicuous inconsistent inculcated incredible incredulous indebted indecent indecisive indefinite independent indicted indifferent indignant indoctrinated indulgent industrious ineffective inept infallible infantilised infatuated inferior inflated influenced influential informed infuriated infused ingenious ingenuous inhibited inhospitable inimical innocent innovative inquisitive insane insatiable insecure insensitive insignificant insincere insistent inspired isolated insufficient insolent insouciant instilled instructive insulted intense interested interfered with interrogated interrupted intimate intimidated intolerant intrepid intrigued introspective introverted intruded upon intrusive invalidated invigorated invisible invited inviting involved invulnerable irrational irresponsible irritated irked

J

jaded jaundiced jealous jeered jeopardised jerked around jilted jinxed jittery jolly jolted jovial joyful joyous jubilant judged judgmental judicious jumpy just justified

K

keen kidded kind kindly kinky knowledgeable

L

labelled lackadaisical laughed at lambasted languid late lavished lax lazy lectured to leery left out legitimate lethargic let down liable liberated lied to lifeless light-hearted likeable liked listened to listless loathed loathsome logical lonely loose lorded over lost loud lousy loveable loved loving lucky lured lust lustful lynched

M

mad malevolent malicious malignant maligned manageable managed managerial manic maniacal manipulable manipulated married maternal mature meagre mean mechanical mediocre medicated meditative melancholic melancholy merry miffed mischievous misdiagnosed miserable miserly misinterpreted misrepresented mistaken mistreated misunderstood misused mixed-up mocked modest molested mollified monopolised moody moralistic morose mothered motherless motivated mournful moved mushy muzzled mystified

N

naive naked nannied narcissistic nasty nauseated needed needled needy negated negative neglected nettled nervous neurotic neutral nihilistic nonchalant noncommittal nonplussed nostalgic noticed numb numbed

O

obeyed obedient objectified obligated obliterated oblivious obscene obsessed obsessive obstructed obvious odd offended old one-upped open opportunistic opposed oppressed optimistic opulent organised ornery ostracised ousted out of balance out of control out of place out of sorts out of touch out of tune outdone outnumbered outraged outranked overcome overdrawn overestimated overjoyed overloaded overlooked overpowered overwhelmed overworked overwrought owed owned

P

pain pained pampered panic panicky paralysed paranoid passed-over passionate passive paternal pathetic patient patronised peaceful peeved pensive perfect peripheral perky perplexed persecuted perturbed perverted pessimistic pestered petrified petulant peeved peevish petty philanthropic phoney picked apart picked on pierced pigeon-holed pious pissed off placated plagued playful pleased pliant pompous poor popular possessionless possessive positive pouty potty powerful powerless practical praised preached to precocious preoccupied pressured pretentious preyed upon primal private privy proactive probed productive promiscuous propagandistic propagandised prosaic prosecuted prosperous protected protective proud provincial provoked prudish psychotic pulverised punished put out put upon pure purposeful pushy put down put out puzzled

Q

quarantined quashed queasy queer querulous questioned quiescent quiet quirky quivery quixotic

R

railroaded rambunctious raped rated rational ravenous reactive reassured realistic rebellious reborn rebuffed rebuked recalcitrant receptive reckless reclusive recognised reconciled redeemed reflective refreshed regret regretful rejected rejecting rejuvenated relaxed released reliable relieved reluctant reminiscent remiss remorse renewed repelled repentant replaceable replaced replenished repressed reproached reproved repulsed rescued resented resentful reserved resigned resistant resolute resourceful respected respectful responsible responsive rested restive restless restrained restricted rueful ruined ruled revengeful revered reverent revitalised revolted rich ridden ridiculed ridiculous right rigid robbed robust romantic rotten rueful rushed

S

sabotaged sacrificed sacrificial sacrilegious sad safe sanctimonious sane sardonic sassy satisfied saved scared scarred scattered scolded scorned scornful screwed scrutinised secure seduced seductive self-absorbed self-acceptant self-assured self-centred self-confident self-conscious self-destructive self-expressed self-indulgent self-rejection self-reliant self-righteous self-sacrificing selfish sensitive sentenced sentimental serene serious set up sexy shadowed shallow sharp shamed shaken sheepish shocked shouted at shunned shut out shy sick significant silenced silly sincere sinful singled-out sceptical skilled skilful slandered slighted sluggish small smart smothered smug snapped at sociable social soft-hearted solemn soothed sophisticated sophomoric sorry spastic special spellbound spent spirited spiteful splendid spoiled spooked spunky squashed squeamish squelched stained stereotyped stepped-on stifled stimulated stingy stomped on stonewalled strained strangled stretched stressed stricken strong stubborn studious stumped stunned stunning stupefied stupid subdued subjugated submissive subordinated subservient successful suicidal suffocated sulky sullen sullied sunk super superb superior supported suppressed sure surly surprised surrendered surveyed susceptible suspicious sympathetic

T

tainted taken aback taken advantage of taken for granted talented talkative tame tantalised tarnished taunted teachable teased tempted tender tense terrible terrified territorial tested testy thoughtful thoughtless threatened thrilled thwarted timid tingly tired titillated tolerant tolerated tormented touched touchy traditional transformed transparent trapped treasured trepidant trespassed tricked triumphant troubled trusted trustworthy tuned-out turned-off turned-on twisted

U

unaccepted unaffected unappealing unappreciated unattractive unavailable unaware uncertain uncivilised uncomfortable uncommitted uncompromising unconfident unconfined unconscious unconsidered unconventional uncultured undaunted undecided undependable underachieving underactualised underestimated undermined underpaid understanding understood under-utilised undervalued underwhelmed undeserving undesirable undesired undisturbed uneasy uneducated unemotional unenlightened unfaithful unfinished unflappable unfocussed unforgettable unforgiven unforgiving unfriendly unfulfilled unhappy unhealed unhealthy unheard unhelped unhelpful unimaginative unimportant unimpressed uninspired uninvited uninviting uninvolved unintelligent uninterested unknown unlovable unloved unmotivated unnecessary unneeded unnerved unpopular unprotected unrealistic unreliable unsafe unsatisfied unskilled unskilful unspoiled unsociable unsocial unstable unsuitable unsullied unsupported unsure untalented unteachable untouchable untouched unwanted unwelcome unworthy unyielding uprooted upset upstaged uptight urgent used useful useless

V

vain validated valued vehement vengeful vexed vicious victimised victorious vigorous vilified violated violent vindicated vindictive virtuous vivacious vulnerable

W

wacky wanted warm-hearted warned warped wary watched weak wealthy weary welcomed wicked wild wise withdrawn wonderful worried worn down worn out worshiped worthless worthy wrong wronged

X

xenophobic

Y

yelled at yielding young young at heart youthful

Z

zany zealous

Feeling Words – How Do You Feel??
© 1995, 1996, 1997, 1998, 1999, Steve Hein

Quiz Answers

Chapter 1: What is emotional intelligence?

1. John Mayer and Peter Salovey.
2. The opposite of emotional intelligence – not being able to focus on feelings.
3. Reuven Bar-On.
4. Robert Thorndike – 1920.
5. No difference on total EQ – women score higher on the 3 interpersonal scales and men score higher on self regard and stress tolerance (Bar-On).
6. Yes, through the right coaching and training.
7. More (Bar-On).
8. See Chapter 1 for my definition of emotional intelligence.
9. Yes, see Chapter 4.
10. Daniel Goleman in his two books *Emotional Intelligence* and *Working with Emotional Intelligence*.

Chapter 2: Underpinning science

1. DHEA.
2. Cortisol.
3. The Heart.
4. Emovare – to move.
5. The Amygdala, referred to here as the 'Emotions Bank'.
6. The Cortex or Neocortex.
7. The Institute of HeartMath.
8. Candace Pert.

Chapter 3: Schools of emotional intelligence

1. Three.
2. Bar-On EQ-i™, MEIS™ and EI-360™
3. Dr. Reuven Bar-On.
4. John Mayer, Peter Salovey & David Caruso
5. Dr. J-P Pawliw-Fry – Institute of Health and Human Potential (IHHP)

6. Bar-On EQ-i™
7. EI-360™
8. MEIS™
9. All of them
10. ECI – see Appendix 3.

Bibliography

Adler, M. (2000). *Quick Fix Your Emotional Intelligence*. Oxford, How To Books.

Alfred, B. B., Snow, C. C. and Miles, R. E. (1996). 'Characteristics of managerial careers in the 21st century'. *Academy of Management Review*, 10, pp. 17–27.

Ashanasy, N. and Tse, B. (1998, August). 'Transformational leadership as management in emotion. A conceptual review.' Paper presented at the First International Conference on Emotions and Organizational Life, San Diego, California, quoted in Rice (2000).

Barling, J., Slater, F., and Kelloway, K. E. (2000). 'Transformational Leadership and Emotional Intelligence: An Exploratory Study', *Leadership and Organization Development Journal*, pp. 157–161.

Barlow, J. and Maul, D. (2000). *Emotional Value: Creating Strong Bonds With Your Customers*. San Francisco, Berrett-Koehler.

Bar-On, R. (1997a). *The Emotional Quotient Inventory (EQ-i) Technical Manual*. Toronto, Multi-Health Systems.

Bar-On, R. (1997b). *The Emotional Quotient Inventory (EQ-i) User's Manual*. Toronto, Multi-Health Systems.

Bar-On, R. (1997b). 'Development of the Bar-On EQ-I: A measure of Emotional Intelligence.' Paper presented at 105th Annual Convention of American Psychological Association, Chicago.

Bar-On, R. (1997c). *The Emotional Quotient Inventory (EQ-i) Administrator's Guide*. Toronto, Multi-Health Systems.

Bar-On, R. (1998). *The Emotional Quotient Inventory (EQ-i) Facilitator's Resource Manual*. Toronto, Multi-Health Systems.

Bar-On, R., Boyatzis, R., Mayer, D. and Caruso, D. (1999). 'Emotional intelligence assessment instruments: Exploring the possibilities with industry experts.' Notes from pre-conference workshop, within Linkage Emotional Intelligence Summit, 27 September 1999, Chicago Marriott Hotel, Chicago.

Bar-On, R. and Handley, R. (1999). *Optimizing People: A Practical Guide for Applying EQ to Improve Personal and Organizational Effectiveness.* Texas, New Braunfels.

Bar-On, R. (2000a). *EQ-i User's Manual.* Revised edition. Toronto, Multi-Health Systems.

Bar-On, R. (2000b). 'Emotional and Social Intelligence: Insights from the EQ-i', in Bar-On, R. and Parker, J. D. A., *The Handbook of Emotional Intelligence.* San Francisco, Jossey-Bass, pp. 363–88.

Bar-On, R. and Parker, J. D. A. (eds) (2000). *The Handbook of Emotional Intelligence.* San Francisco, Jossey-Bass.

Binet, A. and Simm, T. (1916). *The Development of Intelligence in Children.* Baltimore, Williams & Wilkins (original French edition published in 1905).

Block, P. (1981). *Flawless Consulting.* San Diego, Pfeiffer and Company.

Bohm, D. (1996). *On Dialogue.* New York, Routledge.

Boyatzis, R. E. and Goleman, D. in association with Hay/McBer (1999). *Emotional Competence Inventory.* USA, Hay Group.

Branden, N. (1985). *Honoring the Self.* Los Angeles, Jeremy P. Tarcher.

Carter, R. (1999). *Mapping the Mind.* London, University of California Press.

Caruso, D. (1999). *Multi-factor Emotional Intelligence Scaleä (MEISä) Feedback Booklet.* Version 1.1, 19 October. Connecticut, Wolfe and Associates.

Caruso, D. R., Mayer, J. D. and Salovey, P. (in press). 'Emotional intelligence and Emotional Leadership' to appear in R. Riggio and S. Murphy (eds), *Multiple Intelligences and Leadership.* New Jersey, Lawrence Erlbaum Associates.

Caruso, D. and Wolfe, C. J. (2000, September). Workshop Manual, Emotionally Intelligent Certification Workshop. Connecticut.

Cherniss, C. (1999). 'The Business Case for Emotional Intelligence'. Downloadable from www.eiconsortium.org

Cherniss, C. and Adler, M. (2000). *Promoting Emotional Intelligence in Organizations: Make Training in Emotional Intelligence Effective*. Alexandria, Virginia, ASTD.

Childre, D. (1998). *Freeze-frame: One-minute Stress Management*. Boulder Creek, California, Planetary Publishing.

Childre, D. and Cryer, B. (1999). *From Chaos to Coherence*. Woburn, Massachusetts, Butterworth Heinemann.

Childre, D. and Martin, H. (1999). *The HeartMath Solution*. London, Judy Piatkus.

Childre, D. and Watkins, A. D. (work in progress). *The Physiology of Emotions: The Science Connecting Heart and Mind*.

Clark, L. (1997). *SOS Help for Emotions*. Bowling Green, Kentucky, Parents Press.

Clarke, J. (1994). 'SQUIDS', *Sci-American*, August, pp. 46–53.

Cooper, R. K. (1996–1997). *EQ Map*. San Francisco, AIT and Essi Systems.

Cooper, R. K. and Sawaf, A. (1997). *Executive EQ: Emotional Intelligence in Leadership and Organizations.* London, Orion.

Cryer, B. (2000). 'Maximising human performance and organizational intelligence', *Sun Server* magazine. Austin, Texas, Publications & Communications Inc.

Damasio, A. (1994). *Descartes' Error: Emotion, Reason and the Human Brain.* New York, Gusset, Putnum.

Damasio, A. (1999). *The Feeling of What Happens: Body and Emotion in the Making of Consciousness.* Orlando, Harcourt.

Darwin, C. (1872, 1965). *The Expression of Emotions in Man and Animals.* Chicago, University of Chicago Press.

Dekker, J. M., Schouten, E. G., Klootwijk, P., Pool, J., Swenne, C. A., Kromhouse, D. (1997). 'Heart rate variability from short electrocardiographic recordings predicts mortality from all causes in middle-aged and elderly men – the Zutphen study', *American Journal of Epidemiology*, Vol. 145, No. 10, pp. 899–908.

Dulewicz, V. and Higgs, M. (1998). 'Emotional intelligence: managerial fad or valid construct?' Working Paper Series. Henley, Henley Management College.

Ekman, P. (1973). *Darwin and Facial Expression: A Century of Research in Review*. New York, Academic Press.

Elias, M., Tobias, S. and Friedlander, B. (1999). *Emotionally Intelligent Parenting*. London, Hodder and Stoughton.

Forgas, J. 'Handbook of Affect and Social Cognition', chapter in *Emotion, Intelligence, Emotional Intelligence*.

Freedman, J. M., Jensen, A. L., Rideout, M. C., Freedman, P. E. (1997, 1998). *The Handle With Care Emotional Intelligence Activity Book*. San Mateo, California, Six Seconds.

Gallagher, K. (1997). 'Say Cheese'. Unpublished dissertation submitted for BA (Hons) degree, University of Hertfordshire, School of Art and Design.

Gardner, H. (1993). *Frames of Mind*. New York, Basic Books.

Gasson, I, (2000). From research undertaken for Masters in Education degree at Manchester University.

Gellatly, A. and Zarate, O. (1999). *Introducing Mind and Brain*. Cambridge, Icon Books.

Gibbs, N. (1995). 'The EQ Factor', *Time*, 2 October, pp. 60–8.

Glennon, W. (2000). *200 Ways to Raise a Boy's Emotional Intelligence*. Berkeley, California, Conari Press.

Goleman, D. (1985). *Vital Lies, Simple Truths: The Psychology of Self-deception*. New York, Simon and Schuster.

Goleman, D. (1995). *Emotional Intelligence*. London, Bloomsbury.

Goleman, D. (1998a). 'What makes a leader?', *Harvard Business Review*, 76, pp. 93–102.

Goleman, D. (1998b). *Working with Emotional Intelligence*. New York, Bantam Books.

Goleman, D. (2000). 'Leadership that gets results', *Harvard Business Review*, pp. 78–90.

Gottman, J. (1997). *The Heart of Parenting: How to Raise an Emotionally Intelligent Child*. New York, Simon and Schuster.

Handley, R., Caruso, D., Tredwell, B., Jacobs, R. and Orioli, E. (2000). 'Exploring the possibilities with industry experts', handout on emotional intelligence assessment instruments, Pre-summit workshop during Linkage Emotional Intelligence Summit, 10 October, Chicago.

Hedlund, J. and Sternberg, R. J. (2000). 'Too Many Intelligences? Integrating Social, Emotional & Practical Intelligence', chapter in Bar-On, R. and Parker, J.D.A. (eds), *The Handbook of Emotional Intelligence*. San Francisco, Jossey-Bass.

Hughes, R. (2000). 'The impact of emotions at work', *Counselling at Work Journal*, Autumn, 30, Association for Counselling at Work, Rugby, pp. 7–9.

Kravitz, S. M. and Schubert, S. D. (2000). *Emotional Intelligence Works: Developing 'People Smart' Strategies*. Menlo Park, California, Crisp Learning.

Ledoux, J. (1988). *The Emotional Brain: The Mysterious Underpinnings of Emotional Life*. New York, Phoenix.

Leuner, B. (1966). 'Emotional intelligence and emancipation', *Praxis der Kinderpsychologie und Kinderpsychiatrie*, 15, pp. 193–203.

Lewkowicz, A. B. (1999). *Teaching Emotional Intelligence: Making Informed Choices*. Arlington Heights, Illinois, Skylight.

Linkage Incorporated (1999). 'Summit on Emotional Intelligence', conference proceedings book. Conference held at Chicago Marriott Downtown Hotel, Chicago, Illinois, 27–29 September.

Linkage Incorporated (2000a). 'Summit on Emotional Intelligence', conference proceedings book. Conference held at Commonwealth Institute, London, 15–17 May.

Linkage Incorporated (2000b). 'Summit on Emotional Intelligence', conference proceedings book. Conference held at Chicago Marriott Downtown Hotel, Chicago, Illinois, 10–13 October.

McCraty, R., Atkinson, M., Rein, G. and Watkins, A. D. (1996). 'Music enhances the effect of positive emotional states on salivary IgA', *Stress Medicine*, Vol. 12, pp. 167–75.

McCraty, R., Atkinson, M., Tiller, W., Rein, G. and Watkins, A. D. (1995). 'The effects of emotions on short-term power spectrum analysis of heart-rate variability', *The American Journal of Cardiology*. Vol. 76, No. 14, pp. 1089–93.

McCraty, R., Atkinson, M., Tomasino, D. and Tiller, W. A. (1997). 'The electricity of touch: detection and measurement of cardiac energy exchange between people', Proceedings in the Fifth Appalachian Conference on Neurobehavioral Dynamics: Brain and Values, 1996, Radford, Virginia. Mahwah, New Jersey, Lawrence Erlbaum Associates, Inc.

McCraty, R., Barrios-Choplin, B., Rozman, D. and Watkins, A. D. (1998). 'The impact of a new emotional self-management program on stress, emotions, heart-rate variability, DHEA and cortisol', *Integrative Physiological and Behavioural Science*, Vol. 33, No. 2, April–June 1998, pp. 151–70.

Mayer, J. D., Caruso, D. R. and Salovey, P. (1999). 'Emotional intelligence meets traditional standards for an intelligence', *Intelligence*, 27, pp. 267–98.

Mayer, J. D., Caruso, D. R. and Salovey, P. (2000). 'Selecting a measure of emotional intelligence: The case for ability scales' in R. Bar-On and J. D. A. Parker (eds), *The Handbook of Emotional* Intelligence, New York, Jossey-Bass, pp. 92–117.

Mayer, J. D. and Geher, G. (1996). 'Emotional intelligence and the identification of emotion', *Intelligence*, 22, pp. 89–113.

Mayer, J. D. and Salovey, P. (1993). 'The intelligence of Emotional Intelligence', *Intelligence*, 17, pp. 433–42.

Mayer, J. D. and Salovey, P. (1997). 'What is Emotional Intelligence?' in P. Salovey and D. Sluyter (eds), *Emotional Development and Emotional Intelligence: Implications for Educators*. New York, Basic Books, pp. 3–31.

Mayer, J. D., Salovey, P. and Caruso, D. R. (1999a). MSCEIT item booklet – research version 1.1. Toronto, Ontario, Multi-Health Systems.

Mayer, J. D., Salovey, P. and Caruso, D. R. (in press). Manual for the MSCEIT, available from Multi-Health Systems, Toronto, Ontario.

Mayer, J. D., Salovey, P. and Caruso, D. R. (2000). 'Models of Emotional Intelligence' in R.J. Sternberg (ed.), *Handbook of Intelligence* (2nd edn). Cambridge, Cambridge University Press, pp. 396–420.

Mayer, J. D., Salovey, P. and Caruso, D. R. (2000). 'Emotional intelligence as zeitgeist, as personality and as a mental ability' in R. Bar-On and J. D. A. Parker (eds), *The Handbook of Emotional Intelligence*, New York, Jossey-Bass, pp. 92–117.

Orme, G. (1997). 'On being a chameleon' in M. Carroll and M. Walton (eds), *Handbook of Counselling in Organisations*. London, Sage Publications.

Orme, G. (2000). 'The world of emotional intelligence', *Competency and Emotional Intelligence Quarterly*, Vol. 7, No. 3, pp. 23–27.

Orme, G. and Cannon, K. (2000a). 'Everything you wanted to know about implementing an EQ programme. 1: Getting started', *Competency and Emotional Intelligence Quarterly*, London, IRS, Vol. 8, No. 1, pp. 19–24.

Orme, G. and Cannon, K. (2000b). 'Everything you wanted to know about implementing an EQ programme. 2: Design', *Competency and Emotional Intelligence Quarterly*, London, IRS, Vol. 8, No. 2, pp. 17–24.

Orme, G. & Cannon (2001b). 'Getting Started 3: Taking the Show on the Road', *Competency and Emotional Intelligence Quarterly*, Vol. 8, No. 3, pp. 17–24.

Paulhus, D. L., Lysy, D. C., Yik, M. S. M. (1998). 'Self-report measures of intelligence: Are they useful as proxy IQ tests?', *Journal of Personality*, 66, pp. 525–54.

Pert, Candace B. (1997). *The Molecules of Emotions: Why You Feel The Way You Feel*. London, Simon & Schuster.

Plutchik, R. (1984). 'Emotions: A general psychoevolutionary theory' in K. R. Scherer and P. Ekman (eds), *Approaches to Emotion*. Hilsdale, New Jersey, Erlbaum.

Q-metrics (1996). *EQ Map*. San Francisco, California.

Ralston, F. (1995). *Harness Emotional Energy*. New York, Amacom.

Rankin, N. (2000). 'The first Ei summit', *Competency and Emotional Intelligence Quarterly*, London, IRS, Vol. 7, No. 4, pp. 24–8.

Rice, C. L. (1999). 'A quantitative study of Emotional Intelligence and its impact on team performance', unpublished Masters thesis. Malibu, California, Pepperdine University.

Russek, L. G. & Schwartz, G. E. (1996). 'Energy Cardiology: A Dynamical Energy Systems Approach for Integrating Conventional and Alternative Medicine', *Advances*, Vol. 12, No. 4, pp. 4–24.

Ryback, D. (1998). *Putting Emotional Intelligence to Work: Successful Leadership Is More Than IQ*. Woburn, Massachusetts, Butterworth Heinemann.

Ryback, D. (2000). Notes on 'Conflict resolution on relationships' in pre-conference session entitled 'Renewing the deeper self: Emotional intelligence competencies for a lifestyle that works (and plays) well', organized by Linkage 'Emotional intelligence Summit', Chicago, 10 October.

Saarni, C. (1990). 'Emotional competence: How emotions and relationships become integrated' in R. A. Thompson (ed.), *Socioemotional Development*. (Vol. 36, pp 115–82). Nebraska symposium on motivation. Lincoln, Nebraska, University of Nebraska Press.

Saarni, C. (1997). 'Emotional competence and self-regulation in childhood' in P. Salovey and D. Sluyter (eds), *Emotional Development and Emotional Intelligence: Implications for Educators*. New York, Basic Books, pp. 35–66.

Saarni, C. (1999). *The Development of Emotional Competence*. New York, Guilford.

Salovey, P. and Mayer, J. D. (1990). 'Emotional Intelligence', *Imagination, Cognition and Personality*, 9, 185–211.

Salovey, P. and Sluyter, D. J. (eds) (1997). *Emotional Development and Emotional intelligence: Implications for Educators*. New York, Basic Books.

Schwartz, T. (June 2000). 'How do you feel?', *Fast Company Magazine*, pp. 296–313.

Segal, J. (1997). *Raising Your Emotional Intelligence*. New York, Holt.

Shapiro, L. E. (1997). *How to Raise a Child with a High EQ: A Parent's Guide to Emotional Intelligence.* New York, Harper-Perennial.

Sifneos, P. (1972). *Short-Term Psychotherapy and Emotional Crisis.* Harvard University Press, Cambridge, Massachusetts.

Simmons, S. and Simmons, J. C. (1997). *Measuring Emotional Intelligence with Techniques for Self-improvement.* Arlington, Texas, Summit Publishing Group.

Slaski, M. (2000). 'An investigation into emotional intelligence, managerial stress and performance in a UK supermarket chain', unpublished PhD thesis, University of Manchester Institute of Science and Technology.

Song, L. Z. Y. X, Schwartz, G. E. R. and Russek, L. G. S. (1998). 'Heart-focused attention and heart-brain synchronization: Energetic and physiological mechanisms', *Alternative Therapies,* September,. Vol. 4. No. 5. pp. 44–62.

Stein, S. and Book, H. (2000). *The EQ Edge: Emotional Intelligence and Your Success.* Toronto, Stoddart.

Steiner, C. and Perry, P. (1997). *Achieving Emotional Literacy: A Program to Increase Your Emotional Intelligence.* New York, Avon.

Sternberg, R. J. (1996). *Successful Intelligence: How Practice and Creative Intelligence Determine Success in Life.* New York, Simon & Schuster.

Sternberg, R. J. and Smith, C. (1985). 'Social intelligence and decoding skills in nonverbal communication', *Social Cognition,* 3, 168–192.

Strogatz, S. H. and Stewart, I. (1993). 'Coupled oscillators and biological synchronization', *Scientific American.* December, pp. 102–9.

Syrus, Pubilius (1961). 'Sententiae' in J. W. Duff and A. M. Duff (eds), *Minor Latin Poets.* Cambridge, Massachusetts, Harvard University Press (original work published c. 100 BCE).

Thorndike, E. L. (1920). 'A constant error in psychological ratings', *Journal of Applied Psychology,* 4, pp. 25–9.

Thorndike, R. L. and Stein, S. (1937). 'An evaluation of the attempts to measure social intelligence', *Psychological Bulletin,* 34, pp. 275–84.

Tiller, W. A., McCraty, R. and Atkinson, M. (1996). 'Cardiac coherence: A new, non-invasive measure of autonomic nervous system order', *Alternative Therapies*, January, Vol. 2, No. 1. pp. 52–65.

Walsch, N. D. (1995). *Conversations with God. Book 1.* New York, Putnam.

Walsch, N. D. (1997). *Conversations with God. Book 2.* Charlottesville, Virginia, Hampton Roads.

Walsch, N. D. (1998). *Conversations with God. Book 3.* Charlottesville, Virginia, Hampton Roads.

Wechsler, D. (1940). 'Non-intellective factors in general intelligence', *Psychological Bulletin*, 37, pp. 444–5. Reprinted in *Journal of Abnormal Social Psychology*, 38, pp. 100–4.

Wechsler, D. (1958). *The Measurement and Appraisal of Adult Intelligence*, 4th edn. Baltimore, Maryland, The Williams & Wilkins Company.

Weisinger, H. (1998). *Emotional Intelligence at Work.* New York, Jossey Bass.

White, J. and Lehnhoff, L. of HeartMath Institute (2000). Notes from pre-conference session entitled 'The Physiology of Emotional Intelligence: Advancing emotional and organizational intelligence through inner quality management', organised by Linkage for 'Emotional intelligence Summit', Chicago, 10 October.

Whyte, D. (1999). *The House of Belonging.* Langley, Washington, Many Rivers Press.

Wilber, J. (1996). *A Brief History of Everything.* Dublin, Gill & Macmillan.

Yates, M. J. (1997). *CareerSmarts: Jobs With A Future.* New York, Ballantine.

Notes

Chapter 1

[i] The Ei Consortium has created a set of guidelines for training programmes in emotional intelligence. In a series of articles entitled 'Getting started with an EQ programme', the author and Kate Cannon have written about the implementation of the Ei Consortium's guidelines in training programmes to develop emotional intelligence. See bibliography.

[ii] Dr. Linda Pearson's Toronto-based WonderToy company at www.wondertoy.com makes 'Peaches' and 'Babin' dolls, complete with a game and feelings cards to teach children about emotional intelligence. (See Appendix 6.)

[iii] See www.blab.com for greeting cards using I-Feel™ technology.

[iv] Daniel Goleman, in *Emotional Intelligence*, says, 'There is an old-fashioned word for the body of skills that Ei represents: *character.*'

[v] This activity was inspired from information from chapter 12 of *Conversations with God. Book 1* by Neale Donald Walsch.

[vi] From the Bar-On EQ-i technical manual (1997a). The peak at age 49 is partly due to the fact that there are comparatively few people in the sample above aged 60, so in future years, the peak age may be higher as more data is collected.

[vii] Mayer, J.D, Salovey, S. and Caruso, D. (2000), p. 408.

[viii] In his book *CareerSmarts: Jobs with a Future* (Ballantine, 1997) Martin J. Yates listed some 150 different occupations ranging from low to high Ei – this list is reproduced in the MEIS feedback booklet, p. 8.

[ix] Reuven Bar-On in Bar-On, R. and Parker, J. (eds) (2000), p. 367.

[x] IQ was invented in the early 20th Century to determine pupils' fitness for different school programmes. Binet & Simon published the IQ Test in 1905 as a means for calculating a single intelligence score.

[xi] David Wechsler (1940), p. 444.

[xii] See website of the Ei Consortium for 'business case studies' of organisations that have developed emotional intelligence programmes and the results they have achieved. One particularly famous study was conducted by Martin Seligman on Optimism – new recruits to Met Life who scored higher on a 'test of learned optimism' sold 37 per cent more life insurance in their first two years than pessimists (Seligman, 1990, quoted in C. Cherniss, 'The Business Case for Emotional Intelligence.').

[xiii] Hunter Kane Case Studies, 1999–2000, distributed as reference material on Inner Quality Management programmes.

[xiv] Quoted in Hedlund and Sternberg in Bar-On, R., and Parker, J.D.A. (2000), p. 137.

xv Quoted in Bar-On, R. (1997b), p. 6.

xvi Quoted in Bar-On, R. (1997b), p. 6.

xvii Quoted in Bar-On, R. (1997b), p. 6.

xviii Bar-On EQ-i Technical Manual, p. xi.

xix Sternberg, R. J. and Smith, C. (1985).

xx Salovey & Mayer (1990), pp. 185–211.

xxi Story recounted by Dr. Peter Salovey during his keynote speech 'Defining, Measuring and Using Emotional Intelligence' at the Linkage conference, Chicago, October 2000.

xxii *Time*, 2 October 1995.

xxiii Mayer & Salovey (1997), p. 10.

Chapter 2

i Damasio (1994), Damasio (1999), Pert (1997), Childre (1999) and LeDoux (1998).

ii Leeper (1948), p. 17.

iii See Appendix 1 for list of definitions.

iv Pert (1997), p. 189.

v Keynote speech by Richard Boyatzis during pre-conference workshop on assessment instruments. Linkage Incorporated, Ei Summit, Chicago, September 1999.

vi Carter (1998), p. 135.

vii Mayer, Salovey and Caruso (2000) p. 400.

viii Description from 6 seconds website, authored by Josh Freedman.

ix Description here adapted from Joshua Freedman's 'The Hijacking of the Amygdala'.

x Ledoux during radio interview 'Gray Matters: Emotions and the brain' with Garrick Utley. p. 10, transcript.

xi Ledoux during radio interview 'Gray Matters: Emotions and the brain' with Garrick Utley. p. 10, transcript.

xii Quoted by Robert Rand during radio interview 'Gray Matters: Emotions and the brain' with Garrick Utley. p. 6, transcript.

xiii Quoted by Robert Rand during radio interview 'Gray Matters: Emotions and the brain' with Garrick Utley. p. 7, transcript.

xiv Quote by Damasio from transcript of the radio program 'Grey Matters: Emotions and the Brain' with Garrick Utley. p. 4.

xv Quoted in Childre & Martin (1999), p. 30.

xvi Information provided by Dr. Alan Watkins.

xvii Cryer (2000).

xviii Damasio (1994), Chapters 2 and 3.

xix Reported by E.J. Mundell, Reuters Health (internet news), 13 December 2000.

xx Watkins, A (2001). Working title 'The Science Book'. Chapter 1, p. 11 quoted with permission.

xxi Watkins, A (2001). Working title 'The Science Book'. Chapter 1, p. 11 quoted with permission.

xxii FREEZE-FRAMER emotional management enhancer – see list in Appendix 5.

xxiii FREEZE-FRAMER software – see Appendix 5 list of resources.

xxiv The techniques are called Freeze-Frame®, Neutral, intuitive listening and Heart Lock-In®.

xxv HeartZones, available from www.heartmath.com

xxvi McCraty, R., Atkinson, M., Rein, G & Watkins, A.D. (1996). P. 167.

xxvii Cryer, B (2000) 'Maximising human performance and human intelligence'.

xxviii Childre & Martin (1999), p.55

xxix Psychosomatic Medicine. 2000: 62: 623–632.

xxx Pert, C.B. (1997), p. 268–271.

xxxi McCraty, R., Atkinson, M., Tomasino, D. and Tiller, W.A. (1997).

xxxii Reported by Keith Mulvihill for Reuters Health (internet news), 10 November 2000.

xxxiii Mayo Clinic Proceedings 2000: 75: 133–134, 140–143 reported by Reuters Health (internet news), 9 February 2000.

xxxiv Various reports on ReutersHealth.com dated 21 November 2000, 14 July 1999, 28 April 1999 and 20 January 1999 respectively.

xxxv Reported by Robert Lee Holtz for Reuters Health (internet news), 30 November 2000.

Chapter 3

i Linkage Inc. conference proceedings booklet (2000a), p. 61.

ii The word 'measure' is used to refer to the questionnaire or test or instrument for measuring emotional intelligence.

iii Information provided by Multi-Health Systems, December 2000. The languages are English, Canadian French (used only in Canada), German (used in Germany), Dutch (used in Holland and Flemish-speaking Belgium), American Spanish (used on American continents), Norwegian (used in Norway), Danish (used in Denmark), Finnish (used in Finland), Swedish (used in Sweden), Korean (used in Korea), Czech, Russian, Hebrew, Mandarin Chinese.

iv Reuven Bar-On, in Bar-On and Parker (eds) (2000), p. 364.

ᵛ Bar-On e-mail to the author, 15 December 2000.

ᵛⁱ Descriptions from the Technical Manual of the Emotional Quotient Inventory (EQ-i). Bar-On (1997a).

ᵛⁱⁱ Bar-On (1997b), p. 6.

ᵛⁱⁱⁱ When a sufficient number of people have completed a particular test publisher's instrument (usually 1,000 to 3,000 people), 'norms' are created and published in the documentation materials of the instrument. These show the results that were calculated for each group of people who scored the test in the original research group. The norms are impressive – they provide data on numerous studies so that factors of age, gender and race were taken into account in how EQ results are calculated. There is now extensive data on the EQ ingredients for success in different professions.

ⁱˣ The validity indicators include positive impression, negative impression, consistency and omission rate.

ˣ Paulhus, Lysy and Yik (1998): self-estimates of intelligence correlate 0.15–0.30 with measured ability.

ˣⁱ Daniel Goleman's list of acknowledgements, *Emotional Intelligence* (1996), p. 341.

ˣⁱⁱ Mayer and Salovey (1997), presented by Peter Salovey, Linkage conference keynote speech, Chicago, October 2000.

ˣⁱⁱⁱ Caruso, Mayer and Salovey (2001), p. 4.

ˣⁱᵛ Institute for Health and Human Potential brochure 'EQuip yourself', 2000.

ˣᵛ Goleman (1995), p. 214.

Chapter 4

ⁱ Provided by David Caruso, reproduced with permission.

Chapter 5

ⁱ Within the 'Emotionally Intelligent Workshop', Connecticut, October 2000, facilitated by David Caruso and Chuck Wolfe.

Chapter 6

ⁱ Reported in the 'TV Guide' distributed at Linkage conference, Chicago, September 1999, during Hendrie Wiesenger's keynote presentation 'The Power of Positive Criticism'.

Chapter 8

ⁱ Linkage Ei Summit, Chicago, 10 October 2000: pre-conference workshop on 'Renewing the deeper self: Ei competencies for a lifestyle that works (and plays) well'.

[ii] E-mail from Dr Reuven Bar-On and summarised in *Optimising People*, p. 6.

[iii] Descriptions from Bar-On (2000b), pp. 365–6.

[iv] Quoted during post-conference session, Linkage conference, Chicago, October 2000.

Introduction to Part Three

[i] Reported by Stein and Book (2000), pp. 261–8.

[ii] Descriptions from Bar-On (2000b), pp. 365–6.

[iii] Hughes (2000), p. 3.

[iv] Hughes (2000), p. 3.

Chapter 9

[i] Research by the Forum Corporation on Manufacturing and Service Companies, 1989–1995, quoted by Esther Orioli during pre-conference workshop on assessment, Linkage conference, Chicago, October 2000.

Chapter 10

[i] Rice (1999).

[ii] Rice (1999), p. 91.

[iii] Quoted in Ryback (1998), p. 66.

Chapter 11

[i] Alfred, Snow and Miles (1996), pp.17–27.

[ii] Rice (1999).

[iii] Rice (1999), p. 90.

[iv] Leslie and Van Velsor, 1996, quoted in Cherniss, 2000, p. 6.

[v] Slaski (2000), extract, p. 1

[vi] Quoted in People Management magazine, 'Ei can be enhanced through training', 25 January 2001, p. 11.

[vii] Ashkanasy and Tse (1999).

[viii] Quoted in Rice (1999), p. 46.

Conclusion

[i] Bar-On (2000a), p. 83.

Acknowledgements

This book is the collective work of many people – known and unknown, recognised or soon to be recognised. The following people have made it possible for me to act as a 'spokesperson' for the field of emotional intelligence. I want to thank and acknowledge: **Russell**, for introducing me to the topic of emotional intelligence. Without your encouragement for me to initiate my own research, work in the field of emotional intelligence would have been just another good idea. **My mum** for teaching me unconditional love and **my Dad** for the value of hard work and the evils of mediocrity. Thank you both for supporting my wishes, wild dreams and desires and for being there every step of the way. **Neel Kamal, Suresh and Angelie** for providing me with your own real-life examples of emotional intelligence in every form and for putting up with me during the final stages of producing my manuscript. **Kate Cannon** for your friendship and for sharing your insights and your experiences of implementing emotional intelligence pro-grammes. You are a true pioneer in this field, a model of an emo-tionally intelligent parent and someone of deep commitment. It has been a real privilege to get to know you and your son Kevin. Your work at American Express Financial Advisors and your high standards for implementing emotional intelligence programmes have brought rigour and discipline to my creative efforts. **Emotional intelligence practitioners** around the world who share a deep passion and commitment to this work – particularly Lea Brovedani (of Sagacity, Halifax), J. P. and Elizabeth Pawliw-Fry (of IHHP, Toronto), Margareta Sjölund (of Kandidata, Stockholm) and Steve Hein, an independent researcher through whom I have learned a lot of background on emotional intelligence in a short space of time, and who has given me permission to use his work freely and openly. This book is a good opportunity for continuing dialogue on emotional intelligence with all of you. **My colleagues and clients at Emotional intelligence (UK) Ltd** who provide the day-to-day working environment that has made work in emotional intelligence a reality, particularly my colleague **Alex Bird** who has been there since the very beginning – you have been a great friend and colleague. Your commitment to seeing Ei (UK) grow has been a gift. Thank you for writing the original synopses that were the early steps to get this book into print. **Emma Pace** and **Daren Morley**, who were my first push to write a book four years ago. **Jan Johnston**, my friend and neighbour, for drawing the pictures in this book which bring warmth and love to the concepts mentioned here. **Lea Brovedani, Tomi Komoly, Margaret Bird, Kate Cannon, Dr. Alan Watkins, Faith Ralston and Ravi Tangri** for reading my drafts and advising on detail and structure. **Bridget Shine and Matt Pearce** at Crown House Publishing for your support, encouragement and resolve to bring my first book into print. You provided gentle but firm 'guidance' to meet deadlines. Bryan Burns for your vision for promoting this book. To the following people for permission to use their poems which were written during recent emotional intelligence programmes – **Paul Deemer, Alex Bird, Neil Taylor, Russell Speirs, Melanie Theobald and David Mowat.** I have been touched and moved by the steps that you have taken to increase your emotional intelligence. It has been a privilege to walk this journey with you.

All the researchers, psychologists and writers who have helped to put emotional intelligence on the map, including **Daniel Goleman**, who brought this topic to popular attention, **Cary Cherniss** for his excellent work with the Ei Consortium on creating guidelines for successful emotional intelligence programmes, **Jack Mayer, Peter Salovey and David Caruso** for their important work on emotional intelligence as a distinct set of abilities, and **Dr. Reuven Bar-On** for his pioneering and painstakingly hard work over two decades on EQ and the EQ-i. **Bruce Cryer** (of HeartMath Institute, California), **Dr. Alan Watkins** and **Chris Sawicki** (Hunter Kane Resource Management, UK) have made a big contribution to my understanding of the underpinning science and health aspects of emotional intelligence. Your continued work and your commitment to bring scientific and business evidence to this field is a major service to practitioners like myself. A special thank you to **David Caruso** and **Chuck Wolfe** for permission to include example items from the Multifactor Emotional Intelligence Scale (MEIS) in Chapter 4 and to **Dr. Steve Stein and the staff at Multi-Health Systems** who have provided support for our research and use of emotional intelligence measures. To the poet **David Whyte**, I owe the inspiration and courage to use poetry as a vehicle for developing people's emotional intelligence – the poems in this book are a celebration of the value of poetry in helping people connect with their day-to-day life. To all my other teachers, friends, family members and colleagues who remind me constantly that work in the field of emotional intelligence starts and ends with myself. Thank you for your generosity, for challenging me at times when I was 'off track'; you have helped me to discover my purpose. There are too many of you to mention by name. You are all special to me.

Index

EI World

www.eiworld.org

If you would like to be part of a growing world-wide community of people interested in emotional intelligence, please drop an e-mail to:

community@eiworld.org

The EI World website is being created to link together people who wish to:

- share views and opinions about the evolving field of emotional intelligence
- access resources in the field of emotional intelligence and keep up-to-date on new developments in the world of emotional intelligence
- contribute addresses of websites that are in addition to those provided here.

Please send your full contact details in the e-mail and we will keep you posted on news from around the world.